The Grail Legend is a true myth, born in the Middle Ages, when Western civilization was still taking shape. During those times, the collision between values in Christian myths and values in older Celtic/Teutonic myths eventually synthesized in the mythical story of a man in search of the Grail Castle.

Carl G. Jung underlined the importance of the Grail myth since it arose simultaneously—albeit with varying elements—in cultures throughout Medieval Europe; thus, themes from Paganism, Christianity, and Oriental mysticism infuse the stories and heroes born of the Grail Legend. From the universal collective unconscious also emerged four male archetypes, identified by Jungians as Warrior/Hero; Lover; Magician/Wise Man; and King/Father. Using Celtic interpretations of the Grail Legend, *The Grail Castle* provides methods for a man to arouse the four male archetypes within him. *The Grail Castle* then guides men on an exploration of each role to a destination of self-discovery.

Celtic tradition stressed an intense relationship between humans, magic, and nature—a relationship often lacking in contemporary Western culture. Celtic heroes come to us bereft of their fathers, fascinated by womankind, and longing for the Otherworld. For these reasons and more, Celtic stories are genuinely relevant to both men's and women's understanding of today's male.

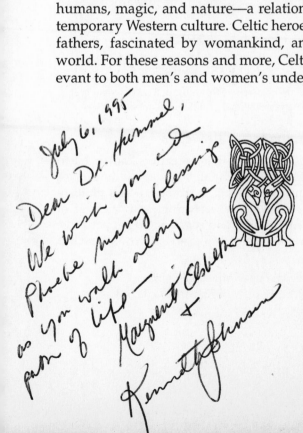

July 6, 1995

Dear Dr. Hummel,

We wish you &
Phoebe many blessings
as you walk along the
path of life—

Marguerite Elsbeth
&
Kenneth Johnson

About the Authors

Kenneth Johnson holds a degree in Comparative Religions with an emphasis on the study of mythology. He is the co-author of *Mythic Astrology* (Llewellyn, 1993). Born in Southern California, he has lived in Los Angeles, Amsterdam, London, and New Mexico. He is currently working on a novel of ancient Europe, entitled *Spirit Riders*.

Marguerite Elsbeth is a professional astrologer and Tarot reader with more than twenty years experience. She has published many articles in magazines such as Dell's *Horoscope* and *The Mountain Astrologer*. A hereditary strega, she also searches for her roots in the Native American tradition. Marguerite is currently working on a novel of contemporary New Mexico, entitled *Hawk*.

To Write to the Authors

If you wish to contact the authors or would like more information about this book, please write to the authors in care of Llewellyn Worldwide and we will forward your request. Both the authors and publisher appreciate hearing from you and learning of your enjoyment of this book and how it has helped you. Llewellyn Worldwide cannot guarantee that every letter written to the authors can be answered, but all will be forwarded. Please write to:

Kenneth Johnson and Marguerite Elsbeth
c/o Llewellyn Worldwide
P.O. Box 64383-K369, St. Paul, MN 55164-0383, U.S.A.

Please enclose a self-addressed, stamped envelope for reply, or $1.00 to cover costs.
If outside U.S.A., enclose international postal reply coupon.

Free Catalog from Llewellyn

For more than 90 years Llewellyn has brought its readers knowledge in the fields of metaphysics and human potential. Learn about the newest books in spiritual guidance, natural healing, astrology, occult philosophy and more. Enjoy book reviews, new age articles, a calendar of events, plus current advertised products and services. To get your free copy of the Llewellyn's New Worlds of Mind and Spirit, send your name and address to:

Llewellyn's New Worlds of Mind and Spirit
P.O. Box 64383-K369, St. Paul, MN 55164-0383, U.S.A.

Llewellyn's Men's Spirituality Series

The Grail Castle

Male Myths & Mysteries in the Celtic Tradition

Kenneth Johnson
&
Marguerite Elsbeth

1995
Llewellyn Publications
St. Paul, Minnesota 55164–0383, U.S.A.

FIRST EDITION, 1995
First Printing, 1995

Cover art by Anna Marie Ferguson (from *Legend: The Arthurian Tarot*)
Cover design by Anne Marie Garrison
Interior illustrations by Nyease Merlin Somersett
Diagrams by Marguerite Elsbeth

Editing, design, and layout by David Godwin

Library of Congress Cataloging in Publication Data

Johnson, Kenneth, 1952–
    The Grail Castle : male myths & mysteries in the Celtic tradition / Kenneth Johnson and Marguerite Elsbeth.
        p.   cm. — (Llewellyn's men's spirituality series)
    Includes index.
    ISBN 1–56718–369–7
    1. Men—Religious life.   2. Mythology, Celtic.   3. Voyages to the otherworld.   4. New Age movement.   I. Elsbeth, Marguerite, 1953–.
    II. Title.   III. Series.
    BL625.65.J64   1994
    299'.16—dc20   94–42827
                                                                    CIP

Llewellyn Publications
A Division of Llewellyn Worldwide, Ltd.
P.O. Box 64383, St. Paul, MN 55164-0383

Llewellyn's Men's Spirituality Series

In recent times, the inevitable backlash to thousands of years of repressive patriarchy and devaluation of the feminine has led to the re-emergence of women's spirituality and a new respect for the ancient Goddess. Yet now the pendulum seeks balance or equilibrium—not a denial of men and everything male, but a new equality between the sexes.

Men may well and rightly revere the Goddess and seek to restore the lost feminine within themselves. Yet, in the process, they must not lose sight of the positive aspects of their own masculinity. There must be a male partner in the *hieros gamos*, the holy marriage within the psyche.

Llewellyn's Men's Spirituality Series will explore these aspects and the possibilities that exist in today's world for male quests for the sacred and for the restoration of the awe and reverence due to our primordial male gods. Men must now forsake the negative and tyrannical aspects of the sexless gods of the patriarchies and embrace instead the wisdom of Odin, the compassion of Osiris, the justice of Zeus, and the moral strength of Krishna. Neither should we overlook the law-giving leadership of the god of Moses, the mercy and self-sacrifice of Jesus, the call to honor and righteousness made by Muhammad, nor the announcement of the New Aeon by Ra-Hoor-Khuit.

Today, in an age that is witnessing the return of the Goddess in all ways and on all levels, there is also a need to find, and re-define, the God within. Men—and women—need to know and to experience the Divine Masculine as well as the Divine Feminine so that the God, too, may be renewed.

Other Books by Marguerite Elsbeth and Kenneth Johnson:

Forthcoming:

*The Silver Wheel: Female Myths and Mysteries
in the Celtic Tradition*

Other Books by Kenneth Johnson:

Mythic Astrology: Archetypal Powers in the Horoscope (with Ariel
Guttman), 1993

Forthcoming:

The North Star Road: Witchcraft and the Shamanic Tradition
Spirit Riders: A Novel of Ancient Europe

Other Books by Marguerite Elsbeth:

Forthcoming:

Masked Dancing: A Shamanic Approach to Archetypal Theater
Hawk: A Novel of Contemporary New Mexico

Acknowledgements

Kenneth Johnson thanks Dr. Dorothea Kenny and Dr. Otto Sadovsky, both of California State University, Fullerton, his first and best teachers in all things pertaining to Celtic mythology and the lore of ancient European peoples.

Marguerite thanks Rev. Fredda Willis Rizzo for always providing timely and appropriate spiritual nourishment, and Dell's *Horoscope* Editors-in-Chief past and present, Julia A. Wagner and Ronnie Grishman, for their willingness to chance her work.

They both thank Carl Llewellyn Weschcke, Nancy Mostad, David Godwin, and all the Llewellyn staff for encouraging and accepting this book; Nyease Merlin Somersett for providing the illustrations; Christine Le May for her moral support and flattering photographic skills; Anna Huserik, for trading her healing touch; Sharon Schenck, for being Santa Fe's only kind-hearted rug merchant extraordinairre; Dr. Bob and his New Age fuel injections; Leise Sargent, for helping us in times of need; Barbara Gage, for her gentle persuasion; and "Dude", for helping to keep the evil spirits at bay.

Table of Contents

Part One

CHAPTER I

The Grail Castle

The Knight of the Grail has had many names: Galahad, Gawain, Parsifal. In the earliest version of the story, composed by Chretien de Troyes[1] about 1185, he is called Perceval, and he does not set out upon his quest with any intention of seeking the Grail—or anything else, for that matter. He is simply trying to find his way back to the house of his mother, whom he left behind him when he set out to become a knight.

He comes to a stream which lies at the bottom of a hill. On the other side of the river, perhaps, he will find his mother's house. But the river is wide and there is no bridge; he cannot get across.

Then Perceval notices two men in a boat in the midst of the stream. One of them is fishing. Perceval calls out: is there any way to cross the river? The Fisherman answers that there is only his little boat, which will certainly not accommodate Perceval's horse. But Perceval may, if he chooses, pass the night at the Fisherman's house. "Go to the top of the hill," the Fisherman tells him, "and there you will see my house."

At first Perceval sees nothing; he is angered, thinking the Fisherman has deceived him. But then he spies a tower rising before him. He approaches it. The Fisherman's home is, in fact, a glorious castle. When Perceval enters, he finds the Fisherman reclining on a couch in the main hall, garbed in royal clothing. The Fisherman excuses himself for not rising to greet his guest; he is ill and cannot get up easily. Perceval sits beside him, and the two begin to talk. Then a squire enters and presents the Fisherman with a sword. This sword has been sent by the Fisherman's niece, and it is a magic sword. There are only three like it in the world, and the smith who made it will die before he can make another. The sword itself will only break in a particularly perilous situation—a situation known only to its maker. The niece's message to the Fisherman is that he may bestow this sword wherever he pleases. He gives it to Perceval.

As Perceval continues his conversation with the Fisherman, another squire enters, passing silently through the hall. He carries a white lance with a white point, and from that point drips a single drop of red blood. After the lance has passed by, a beautiful damsel enters, carrying a gold cup or grail encrusted with jewels. Then another damsel passes by, carrying a silver serving dish. Perceval longs to know the meaning of all this. He especially wants to know why the lance drips with blood and who is to be served with the grail cup. But his mentor in the arts of chivalry, an old knight named Gornemant, had told him never to ask too many questions. So Perceval says nothing.

A table is brought into the hall—a magic table which can never rot, made of black ebony and covered with a white cloth. A grandiose feast follows. But throughout the feast, upon several occasions, the damsel can be seen to pass through the hall, carrying the grail. Still Perceval longs to ask: whom does the grail serve? But still he remains silent, resolving to ask one of the squires in the morning.

At the end of the feast, the Fisherman is carried away by his servants and Perceval is shown to his own room. He wakes in the morning, the sun already risen. No one comes to help him dress. So he puts on his own clothes and ventures forth into the castle. It is

Perceval Approaches the Grail Castle

empty. He knocks on doors. There is no answer. He finds his way into the courtyard; his horse is saddled and his weapons are waiting for him. He mounts; the drawbridge is open, so he rides out, hoping to find the Fisherman and his retinue hunting in the woods. But the bridge begins to rise just as Perceval is crossing it; only a leap of his horse lands him safely on the other side of the moat. The drawbridge slams shut. Perceval calls out: Who has raised the bridge? Who is there? But he receives no answer.

And so Perceval goes on his way alone. Before long, he comes upon a young woman weeping in the forest, holding the body of a knight, her slain lover, in her lap. The conversation which follows seems to make little sense, at least in a practical way. After only a passing remark about her dead knight, the lady comments that Perceval's horse seems well curried and cared for, yet there is no lodging place within many days travel from this spot. Perceval tells her of the castle in which he has spent the previous night. The woman replies: "Then you were at the house of the rich Fisher King."

Perceval had been unaware that his host was, in fact, a king. The damsel proceeds to tell him the whole story: how the king was wounded in the thigh with a javelin and can scarcely walk. Unable to ride, his only pastime is fishing. The country round about the Grail Castle is in a state of blight or decay because of the king's wounds.

The damsel now asks Perceval about his experiences. Did he see the bleeding lance? The woman carrying the grail? Did he see the silver serving dish? Perceval replies in the affirmative. The damsel continues: Did Perceval ask any questions? Did he ask why the lance was bleeding, or whom the grail serves? Perceval confesses that he did not.

The damsel rages at him, cursing his stupidity. If he had followed his natural curiosity rather than the instructions of his mentor, the Fisher King would have been restored by the very asking of those questions. But thanks to Perceval's silence, barrenness will continue to rule in the Grail Kingdom. Furthermore, the damsel reveals that she knows who he is, that she is in fact his cousin, and that she has news of his mother. She is dead: she died of grief when Perceval rode off to become a knight.

So the very nature of Perceval's quest has changed. He is no longer seeking his mother, whom he has lost forever. Now he must search for the Grail Castle once again. He must find the magic path back to that Otherworldly spot, and ask the questions which will heal the land.

Unfortunately, Chretien de Troyes died before he could finish his tale. He never brought Perceval back to the Grail Castle. But other writers took up the story. The Grail became one of the great themes of medieval literature. And different writers found different roads back to the Grail Castle. In the following pages, we shall attempt to find still others.

Where did the Grail Legend come from? Its sources are many. Though the medieval versions of the story are filled with Christian symbolism—the lance is the spear that pierced Christ's side and the grail itself the cup from which He drank at the Last Supper—it is clear that the legend has its origins in pagan Celtic myth. The old Irish sagas tell of the Four Treasures which the Tuatha de Danaan, the Children of the Goddess Danu, brought with them to Ireland—the sword of Nuada, the spear of Lugh, the cauldron of the Dagda, and the stone of Fal, which cried out whenever a true king placed his foot upon it. These magical items are easily recognizable as Perceval's sword, the bleeding lance, the grail, and the silver platter respectively. Anyone acquainted with the Tarot will also recognize the four suits of the Minor Arcana: Wands (the spear), Cups (the grail), Swords (the sword), and Pentacles (the platter). And those who are familiar with the general contours of Celtic mythology might also recall the theme of the journey to the Otherworld, Tir-na-nog, the Land of Youth, and may note that Perceval's journey to the Grail Castle bears all the marks of being yet another classic venture into that realm.[2]

But during the Middle Ages, other influences were brought to bear on this Celtic vision quest. Many of the knights who went crusading in the East were deeply influenced by Gnostic and Sufi doctrines there. They returned to Europe bringing these influences with them—influences which inspired the Knights Templar, the heretical Cathars of southern France, and the Troubadour poets with their songs of divine and earthly love. These Gnostic and Oriental themes also found their way into the Grail story. Chretien de Troyes himself worked and wrote at the court of Marie de Champagne, a patroness of the Troubadours; her mother, Eleanor of Aquitaine, literally owned most of the Cathar heartland in the south.

The Grail Legend is a true myth, one in which various themes from paganism, Christianity, and Oriental mysticism all combine, and which was the common currency of many writers rather than the product of any one man's vision. Carl Jung felt that the Grail Legend was vitally important to us all because it is the most recent of the great myths to emerge from the collective unconscious. It arose during the Middle Ages, when Western civilization was still taking shape, and as such it constitutes the primary myth of that civilization. Historically, it represents a collision of values: the Christian myth collided with older Celtic and Teutonic myths, and the collective imagination of mankind shaped a new synthesis: the Grail Legend.

Our principal concern here, however, is with what that myth tells us about men and their journey through life. Let's go back to the beginning of our story, and examine the mythic or spiritual meaning behind Perceval's quest.

Much like a man who has completed his time of military service and is in the process of returning to his home and family, Perceval seeks to return to the house of his mother after doing service at King Arthur's court and winning his knighthood. There is an aura of aimlessness about Perceval's journey, almost as if he is returning home for lack of anything better to do. Perceval knows he is missing something, a part of himself that is not yet clearly defined in his consciousness. He is compelled onward by his feeling nature. One wonders just how much he has remained in touch with this side of himself—the passive, subjective side—after spending so much time in the company of warriors.

He comes to a stream he cannot cross. Water is a universal symbol of the unconscious mind, a region where logic and objective reasoning must defer to deduction and sensory experience. This stream of unconsciousness is difficult to cross if we have become separated from our feelings and our ability to flow in oneness with our surroundings. The two men fishing in the stream cannot help

Perceval cross the water, but they kindly offer him a night's lodging in their house on the hill. This "house" proves to be a castle—the Grail Castle itself.

That the Grail Castle represents a state of mystic unity with all things is apparent from its symbolism. In Eastern religions, the spiritual aspirant makes use of a diagram called a mandala, which symbolizes both the cosmos at large and the miniature cosmos of the human psyche. A typical mandala is circular in form, though it usually includes a square or some other fourfold figure as well. Meditation upon the mandala helps guide the meditator towards that state of oneness which the mandala represents.

But mandalas are not limited to Eastern spiritual techniques. As Jung demonstrated in many of his writings, they are universal. In fact, human beings tend to produce them spontaneously and unconsciously, whether in art, in myth, or in dreams. In the West, the mandala may be imaged as an ideal city or, in alchemical and Kabbalistic works, as a cosmogram, a portrait of the universe. But its components are always the same. The square or cross appears, as does the circle. The mandala unites the circle and the square.[3]

The Grail Castle is clearly a mandala (see illustration on page 11). Because it is surrounded by a moat, it is enclosed by a circular motif, precisely like the mandalas of India and Tibet. And within the castle itself Perceval sees the Four Treasures of the Grail, equivalent to the square or four-armed cross.

But if the Grail Castle represents an experience of mystical unity, then how does that psychological experience make itself felt in the lives of men today?

The Grail Castle is in fact something men possess from the beginning. It is something innate, something known from childhood. Psychologically speaking, the Grail Castle is the source of a man's creativity, his own portion of the magic which animates the world around him. To realize the Grail Castle is to experience enlightenment, at least after a fashion.

In the East, men seek this unity consciously. But with the exception of isolated occultists like the alchemists or the Gnostics, Westerners have tended to blunder into it unconsciously, if at all—just as Perceval comes upon the Grail Castle by accident. This parallels the psychological experience of men everywhere. In his analysis of the Grail myth, psychologist Robert Johnson[4] affirms that most men stumble into the Grail Castle for the first time in childhood or in early adolescence. And they never forget it.

We have all experienced moments of perfection. We may wake to find that sun, curtains, and kitchen smells combine to create a heightened sense of beauty which is very close to a religious experience. We may walk through a patch of woods close to home and be possessed by that oneness with all Nature that the Taoists of ancient China equated with enlightenment. This experience of mystical unity, this blundering into moments of enlightenment, may be brought on by the most ordinary experiences of life. (One of the authors grew up in an environment where it was not uncommon for teenaged boys to have their first "grail moment" on a surfboard.) The grail moment is not a sexual experience. Though Robert Johnson links the grail experience with adolescence,[5] we believe that it can just as easily happen earlier—perhaps much earlier—in a boy's life, well before the advent of sexual consciousness. But whatever it is that plunges a boy into the Grail Castle, those transcendent moments are something which will remain with him for the rest of his life. For a moment he is in paradise. The poet William Wordsworth has left us a masterful description of such perfect moments:

> There was a time when meadow, grove, and stream,
> The earth, and every common sight,
> To me did seem
> Apparelled in celestial light,
> The glory and the freshness of a dream.
> It is not now as it hath been of yore;—
> Turn wheresoe'er I may,
> By night or day,
> The things which I have seen I now can see no more...[6]

Wordsworth's poem brings up a most important point—the Grail Castle is lost. He can no longer see, in the fullness of his adulthood, those things he saw with the magical eyes of childhood.

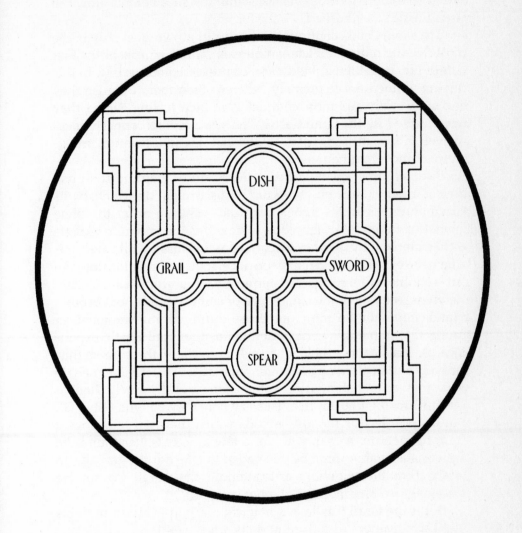

The Grail Castle Mandala

Like Perceval, he has awakened to find the castle empty, the draw-bridge to a more glorious reality slamming shut behind him. The Grail Castle has vanished.

The Grail Castle continues to appear to grown men only in the most fleeting moments. These moments cannot, at least in the first half of life, be retained, held onto, or possessed absolutely. In this respect women are supremely different than men. Because they live more easily and more completely in their feeling nature, they never quite lose the Grail Castle. The sense of interconnectedness with all things, the sense of absolute relatedness, is a natural inheritance of the feminine.

But men must take a different road. All of them must, at one time or another, take up the sword of discrimination which, by its very nature, separates things from each other in order to define them, to differentiate. Hence Jung wrote that the masculine nature is characterized by logos or focused consciousness, while the feminine nature is characterized by eros, i.e. love and relationship.[7] To put it another way: man seeks perfection while woman seeks completeness. Men have the experience of completeness—of absolute relationship with the entire universe—during fugitive moments in youth, the moments we have defined as the Grail Castle experience. A man cannot help but seek to reclaim these moments, furtively and in aloneness, throughout his life. This is what men do when they go on fishing trips, sitting alone and absolutely silent in a boat watching the sun rise. This is where they go when they fall into deep reflective moods—moods which their wives or lovers cannot penetrate. A man who, for a few moments, has found the Grail Castle again cannot be persuaded to take out the garbage, to gossip about the neighbors, or to attend to the charge account. He is basking in a rare moment of inner splendor.[8]

But if the Grail Castle is a magical place, it is also a perilous one. Daydreamers and drug addicts alike seek the Grail Castle, and with too great a fervor. There are times when a man *should* return to earth long enough to take out the garbage or attend to the charge account. But instead he lingers in the Grail Castle, like a Celtic hero lost in the barrows of the fairy folk for a hundred years or more.

To experience the grail in childhood is to gain an intimation of that state of perfect union with all things which may also be defined as enlightenment, dwelling in the center of the mandala. The search to regain the grail is the quest, the only true quest. But if we linger in our childhood cloud castles the quest may turn sour and fruitless. Instead we must approach the castle again as fully conscious adults who, like an older and wiser Perceval, are prepared to ask the right questions. No one does this by remaining locked in the grail world of childhood.

This is why it is imperative—absolutely essential—that a man must lose the Grail Castle. The loss of the inner grail is itself a fundamental stage of the quest. For it is the loss of the grail which opens for men the sacred wound, and makes all of them Fisher Kings. The loss of the childhood grail world sets each man upon his personal, solitary road through the forest. He may follow one, or perhaps two, of four great paths: that of the Warrior, the Lover, the Magician or the King.[9] These are the paths symbolized by the Four Grail Treasures.

As we noted earlier, these Four Treasures are potent symbols which have their roots in ancient Celtic mythology. They also represent four paths, four roads upon which men may travel to reach the Grail Castle, four modes of being which govern and shape men's lives. These Four Treasures lie at the heart of our own personal Grail Quest, the quest which is the real subject of this book.

The powerful importance attached to these Four Treasures raises a fundamental question: Why is the circle of wholeness always linked with the four-cornered square? Why this insistence upon the number four?

Almost all of the world's great spiritual traditions hold the number four in special regard. Native Americans base the Medicine Wheel on the cross of the four directions (another union of circle and square). Buddhist and Hindu mandalas, as we have noted, are also based upon the circle and square. The pottery of Neolithic Europe, c. 5000 BC, frequently depicts a cross which probably represents the four directions or the four seasons. The horoscope diagram in astrology is a circle divided into four quadrants by a cross, and each sign of the zodiac may be classified according to one of the four elements of ancient physics. It is in these four elements that we find the key to the mandala motif of the squared circle.

Jung recognized four functions inherent within the human psyche, corresponding to the four elements of classical Greek physics. These are: intuition (fire), feeling (water), thinking (air) and sensation (earth).[10] Typically, an individual relies on one—or, at the most, two—of these functions in his or her daily life. This leaves us all a little bit one-sided. To harmonize and balance all four elements, all four functions of the psyche, is to achieve a wholeness which unites us with the universe at large. We are no longer separate and discrete units, isolated from the world around us. We are whole. The alchemists sought the "quintessence," a unified field comprised of all four elements. When we bring the four quarters and the four directions of reality and consciousness together into a unity or quintessence, we create the circle, symbol of completeness. This is the meaning of the mandala. This is what the Grail Castle is all about. The Four Treasures of the Grail, no matter where they may have come from historically, are the four elements or four functions of the human psyche: intuition (the lance), feeling (the grail), thinking (the sword) and sensation (the platter). Inasmuch as both men and women rely upon one or two of these four functions as a guidepost or path for everyday life, the Four Grail Treasures may be taken as emblematic of the four essential archetypes or roads to wholeness which we have already defined as the paths of the Warrior (the sword of intellect), Lover (the cup of feelings), Magician (the wand of intuition) or King (the pentacle of sensation).

Therefore it will be worthwhile, even essential, to examine these Four Treasures at some length. In so doing, we shall make use of the technique of symbolic amplification—which simply means that we shall allow the various symbolic meanings attached to each Grail Treasure to speak for themselves, to interact with each other, and to crystallize into a core of psychological meaning. The symbolism itself is drawn partly from the mythologies of the Western world and partly from Western spiritual disciplines such as alchemy, Kabbalah, and Hermetic philosophy, all of which gave very definite and specific meanings to the ancient myths.

In the chapters which follow, we shall (for the moment, at least) leave Perceval to his own quest, wandering through the forest, and

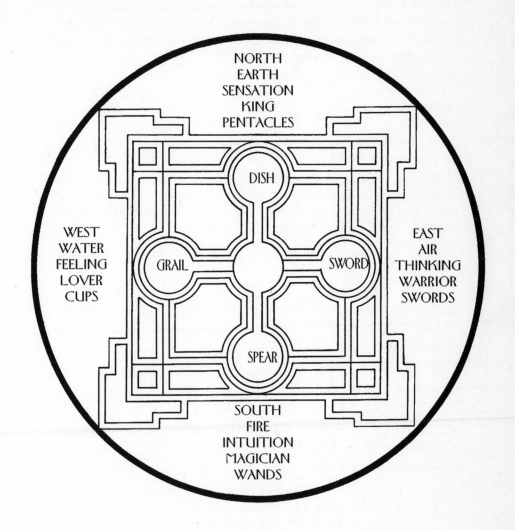

The Four Grail Treasures

instead we shall follow each of the four paths for a time, for each path leads ultimately back to the Grail Castle. We shall also provide a series of guidelines and a test to assist you, the reader, in identifying which of these four archetypes is most deeply alive within you.

We all need to do this for ourselves. Like Perceval, most of us have never received a proper initiation.

Notes

1. "Perceval," in Loomis, Roger Sherman, and Laura Hibbard, eds., *Arthurian Romances* (New York: Random House, 1957), 3–87.

2. Alfred Douglas, *The Tarot* (Harmondsworth: Penguin, 1972), 37–8; Emma Jung and Marie-Louise von Franz, *The Grail Legend* (New York: G. P. Putnam's Sons, 1970), 9–38; and Proinsias MacCana, *Celtic Mythology* (London: Hamlyn, 1973), 132.

3. Carl Jung, "Mandala Symbolism," in *The Archetypes and the Collective Unconscious* (Collected Works, vol. 9, part I) (Princeton: Princeton University Press, 1977), 355–90.

4. Robert Johnson, *He: Understanding Masculine Psychology* (New York: Harper & Row, 1977).

5. Ibid., 7–14.

6. William Wordsworth, "Ode: Intimations of Immortality from Recollections of Early Childhood," in W.H. Auden and Norman Holmes Pearson, eds., *Romantic Poets* (New York: Viking Press, 1969), 197.

7. C.G. Jung, "The Phenomenology of the Self," in *The Portable Jung*, ed. Joseph Campbell (New York: Viking Penguin, 1980), 148–62.

8. Johnson, op. cit.

9. These four types were originally the creation of Jungian psychologist Toni Wolff (see Edward C. Whitmont, *The Symbolic Quest* [New York: Harper & Row, 1973], 178–84). They also form the focus of Robert Moore and Douglas Gillette, *King, Warrior, Magician, Lover: Rediscovering the Archetypes of the Mature Masculine* (San Francisco: HarperSanFrancisco, 1990).

10. Jung, "Psychological Types," in *The Portable Jung*, 178–269.

CHAPTER 2

The Warrior

The Warrior is a fitting archetype with which to begin, for no male role has been so highly praised or so deeply maligned. Scarcely a male child exists who, at one time or another, has not longed to grow up to be the hero, the knight, the "good soldier." But even though all men possess an inner Warrior upon whom they may call in times of need, few men are born to play the hero's role as their principal mode of life. The Warrior's path is the loneliest of all—he dwells in a suit of armor, symbolizing his inner isolation; that's just his way. This is why the Old Western gunslinger—one of America's favorite Warrior archetypes—must ride into town *alone* and, having fought for the good of the people, *leave* town *alone*—saying farewell to the women who have learned to adore him. In the end, only the sunset may claim him.

This sense of inner isolation is poignantly expressed in the sweet-sung words of "Desperado," a song from the 1970s written by the (aptly named) band, the Eagles, wherein it is suggested that the warrior-outlaw should wake up and smell the coffee, come down from his high horse (so to speak), and acknowledge his feeling self.[1] But that would have been a tall order for the likes of Jesse James or John Wesley Hardin. And what about Clyde Barrow or Pretty Boy Floyd? Surely these 1930s mobsters would have been cheerfully able to recognize and clean up the outworn garbage of their repressed emotions! Maybe that's what they were trying to do when they went out on a killing spree. Maybe sociopathic behavior is a catharsis for the criminally insane. But what does such behavior have to do with the more average Warrior personality, the sports fan or motorcycle enthusiast?

Some have seen the Warrior as a very American *problem*.[2] It is true that we tend to romanticize or deny the grisly activities of today's hardened psychopaths, our Warriors gone mad. Serial killer Ted Bundy had hoards of willing groupies and potential marriage partners, despite the gruesome facts of his case. No one seemed to notice that Jeffrey Dahmer (an armored isolationist in the extreme) kept two huge freezers in his living room and never went out to dinner. And even when dinner escaped to tell the tale, it fell on deaf ears.

These are radical or extreme examples. But they indicate that our society has grown fearful of its feeling nature. People would rather murder, idolize, marry, or ignore their passions than express their feelings in positive, constructive ways. So it is no wonder that we hear, again and again, that we live in a nation which, essentially, produces killing machines, the perversion of the Warrior archetype. And though this may to some extent be true, it is equally true that we have *lost* our Warrior spirit, and that many American men feel disempowered. (Of course, the killing machine is equally disempowered, whether or not he is conscious of the fact.) The "problem" of the Warrior is not limited to American culture. It is a worldwide phenomenon, just as passionately felt by the businessmen of Japan as by those of the United States, by the rebels of Yugoslavia as well as by the U.S. Army. Let us, then, examine what the Grail story—and some of the older Celtic legends upon which it is based—can tell us about the Warrior.

Upon entering the Grail Castle, Perceval is given a magic sword which can only be broken under extraordinarily perilous circumstances. In the Tarot, the suit of Swords represents ambition, boldness, wrath, and war. Swords also indicate transformation and activity and are associated with the element of air. Air symbolizes the *mental plane*. The quality of air alludes to our ability to be alert, to express our curiosity and ideas as well as our intellectuality, perception, and logic. This gives us a not-so-subtle hint that when Perceval was gifted with a sword he was being asked to *think*.

The sword is also a symbol of virility, strength, and manhood. It represents life and death, alluding to a pair of opposites which we may associate with our powers of observation and our ability to discriminate between dark and light, good and evil, right and wrong, Spirit and Matter. The Hebrew word *zain* means "sword" when used as a noun, but "cleave or separate" when used as a verb. Hence the sword separates us from our true self due to our logical (or, more accurately, illogical) interpretations of the shifting world of form. But it can also separate us from illusion and falsehood if we are willing to use our inner swords with enlightened will power and discrimination. Only through the development of this heightened will power can we gain the ability to choose wisely between the opposites, the sacred and profane. The essence of the sword's positive function, then, is simply this: our ability to arrive at a determined decision. But sadly enough, for most of us the sword remains both a wound and the power to wound, symbolic of the great gulf between logic and the Self.

The Warrior, then, is primarily a thinker. This may sound surprising—or even incomprehensible—to some, but it is in keeping with all the mythic symbols. The Warrior's clear and discriminating thinking process is precisely that which creates his sense of isolation, for the mind, like a sword, separates us from unity by making clear distinctions. These distinctions, arising from mind, are expressed through *speech.*

When ancient Celtic warriors brandished their swords against an enemy, they also sounded their battle cry. There is a strong allegorical connection between the sword and the faculty of speech. The sword is a weapon of war, and Mars is the god of war, whether in Greco-Roman myth or in the practice of astrology. Another great symbolic language which emerged from the same matrix as the Grail

Legend was the Kabbalah, and in the Kabbalah the power of *speech* is symbolically linked with the astrological planet Mars. In Kabbalah, sound vibration is the process by which the entire universe is formulated and comes into being. Speech is the power behind the Logos of Hermetic philosophy, the Divine Word which creates.

The power of sound was a weapon of war in the Old Testament as well. During the battle of Jericho, the warriors were told to encompass the city and "when ye hear the sound of the trumpet, all the people shall shout with a great shout; and the wall of the city shall fall down flat..." (Joshua 6:5).

Sound is the sword of our thoughts in action. This tells us that when Perceval receives his sword, he is being told not only to think but also to *speak.* And this, of course, is precisely what he does not do.

All of this provides us with a valuable clue to the Warrior's role in our own world, for the modern Warrior often fights with words. The old adage, "the pen is mightier than the sword," is a tribute to the Warrior's decidedly literary flair, and some male mythologists[3] have correctly noted that a man plays the Warrior whenever he creates. So we should not be surprised to find that in Celtic myth the Warrior and the poet or bard are frequently linked. Perhaps the most powerful example is that of Gwydion, son of Don, who figures in the Fourth Branch of the *Mabinogion.*[4] Though he appears as a "hero" in this medieval collection of Welsh myth and folklore, it is clear that he was once a god, for the Milky Way itself is called Caer Gwydion, Gwydion's Castle. Like the Norse Odin, he was a god of battle as well as the god who knew the magic power of words and the alphabet. In an old Welsh poem called "The Battle of the Trees," Gwydion musters an army of trees to do battle with the forces of Annwn, the Celtic Underworld. As Robert Graves pointed out,[5] these are not just *any* trees. The Celts had a magic alphabet called Ogham; like Norse Runes, the Ogham letters were used for magic and divination as well as for literary purposes. Each letter of the Ogham was associated with a particular tree, and hence with a whole range of related symbols. The trees mustered by Gwydion are the Ogham trees, which is to say that he is employing the magic of words and letters to combat the forces of darkness. In fact, it is not through the medium of his arboreal army that Gwydion defeats the lords of the Underworld, but through guessing the *name* of the Underworld champion (his name is Bran, but that is a story for a later chapter). In mythology, power over the sacred names is the mark of a Druid or Magician.

Whenever a man learns to think, whenever he picks up pen and paper to express himself, he is playing the Warrior. But he must pay a price for the gifts of logic and discrimination. If he is a pure Warrior, he must live out his life in a suit of armor, questing through dark forests and isolated from human warmth. If he is a literary Warrior, he will have to undergo a painful initiation into the realms of knowledge. Odin hung for nine days and nights on the World Tree in order to learn the lore of the Runes. Gwydion likewise suffered magical imprisonment. Another name for this magical bard was Gweir, and an old Welsh poem tells us: "Stout was the prison of Gweir, in Caer Sidi..."[6] The name Caer Sidi means "Revolving Castle," and reminds us of the *mandalic* Grail Castle. In another context, the Underworld prison of King Arthur is called a "bone-fortress," in which he is imprisoned by another magician figure, Manawyddan map Llyr,[7] and this may remind us that Siberian shamans often experience the process of initiation as reduction to a skeletal condition.[8] In all cases, isolation is the keynote of the Warrior, be he knightly or bardic.

When a man loses the Grail Castle of his childhood imagination, he naturally becomes isolated. He has begun the path to manhood. Some types of men, notably the Lover and the Magician, maintain a connection with the unconscious or with the world of the feminine which greatly decreases that isolation and gives these men somewhat easier access to the Grail Castle. But the Warrior is perhaps the most solitary of all men, and his isolation often brings him to grief. The story of Sir Balin, contained in Malory's *Le Morte D'Arthur*,[9] is a brilliant but sad example.

One day a damsel appeared at the court of King Arthur. She had come, she said, from Avalon, and she carried with her a magic sword that was causing her great suffering and travail. Only a pure knight could bring forth the sword from its scabbard. Many attempted the feat, but no one could do it—not even Arthur, whose purity had apparently been compromised somewhat by politics since the famous episode of the sword in the stone. At last, the magic sword was drawn forth by a poor unknown knight named Sir Balin. The feat accomplished, the lady immediately asked Balin to give the sword back to her. But now he possessed a magic sword and was unwilling to give it up. So he refused.

That was the beginning of Sir Balin's troubles. Shortly afterwards, he slew the Lady of the Lake while she was under King Arthur's protection, and got himself banished thereby. So he rode through the world, lonely and isolated, seeking always to do good but forever doing harm. In defending another lady, he found himself in the Grail Castle, where he slew the Grail King's brother in the lady's defense. This brought the Grail King to his feet, sword in hand, and it was Sir Balin who (at least in this version of the story) struck the Grail King his magic wound and created the wasteland. Finally, he came upon his own brother, Sir Balan, but did not recognize him. The two men fought until both were killed, and so ended the sad story of Sir Balin.

What was it that turned Sir Balin's deeds to mischance, no matter how hard he sought to do the right thing? We may remember that his troubles began when he refused to return the sword to the damsel from Avalon. He had refused to honor the feminine or recognize the power of enchantment and imagination in his own life. So quickly had he lost the shining innocence which allowed him to win the sword in the first place.

But how do we lose the innocence and imagination which gives us a power like magic? What makes us forget how to wield our swords as instruments of enchantment rather than war?

For most of us, the sense of isolation which creates our suits of armor is something which began when we were very young. Many Celtic Warrior heroes of old felt the powerful absence of the Father spirit in their lives, and many men of today find themselves in the same situation.

Few Celtic myths describe for us a deep relationship between father and son. In many cases, the father is entirely absent, a dim figure who never appears on the stage. Perceval's father, a knight, was slain years before the beginning of the story, so that Perceval remembers only his forest upbringing with his mother. King Bran and his magical brother Manawyddan, characters in the *Mabinogion,* were the sons of the sea-god Llyr, who never actually appears on the stage of their lives. Finn MacCool lost his father to a war, as did Perceval, and King Arthur's father Uther Pendragon actually gave his son up to be raised in the woods, then proceeded to die during the boy's absence. Merlin's father was the devil (thus giving Merlin reasons to be glad that his father was absent!).

The greatest warrior in the mythology of ancient Ireland was Cuchulain of Ulster, and he too is an excellent case in point. Cuchulain's parentage was much in dispute. Some believed him to be the incestuous child of King Conor mac Nessa of Ulster and his sister Dectera. Others believed him to be the son of the great god Lugh who abducted Dectera into the Otherworld. Dectera married a fellow called Sualtim, but few of the myths allege that he was Cuchulain's father or assign him any kind of a parental role. The greatest of all warriors, then, grew up in his mother's world.

Very well. Whether dear old dad was a sea-god, a slain knight, a high king, the devil, or just a military man, corporate executive, Krishna devotee, or couch potato, the question remains the same for all men: What is the father's legacy? And the answer, all too often, is: none at all.

In their fatherlessness, these Celtic heroes have a special relevance for us in the twentieth century. We, too, suffer from the wounds that open when the father is absent. Many boys now grow up as the children of divorced families, raised by their mothers as was Perceval in the forest, in homes where the father is conspicuously absent. Even if the father is physically present, he is often spiritually absent—tied to a job he despises, gone all day at the office and, at home, intent only upon retreating from his miseries into a makeshift Grail Castle of beer and football. Either way, the typical modern man doesn't get much good "fathering." He might as well be fatherless altogether, for the absence of male power in his life has opened within him a wound which is hard to heal. Some try to heal it with the salt of their tears: the Warrior tries to battle it out of existence. So he learns to pick up a sword.

But what if that sword is broken? Though Perceval's sword is

23

not actually broken, he behaves as if it were. In fact, his magic sword will only break in a situation of great peril, but Perceval himself cannot know exactly what that situation will be. This uncertainty regarding the magic sword would seem to mean that men have to make the right judgment *intuitively* when the time of testing arrives. Logic alone won't tell them when and how their sword of action and empowered speech is likely to break. As well as manifesting the courage of the hero, they have to retain a connection with spirit in order to know when the sword will prevail and when it will shatter. But in a world where most men feel a lack of power— as if their swords had broken long ago, when they were unaware— we must also ask: How can the magic sword be mended? This may turn out to be the same question as: How can the Fisher King be made whole? How can men heal their inner wounds?

In Teutonic myth, the youthful hero Siegfried finds the broken shards of the sword Balmunga, which Odin had given to his father Siegmund. Despite his magic skill, the blacksmith Mime cannot reforge it. In Arthurian legend, Gawain is given a broken sword which he also cannot repair to its original state of wholeness. Are these myths trying to tell us that a man can never be completely healed of his inner wounds? Are all men Fisher Kings, wounded unto death but yet unable to die, thus doomed to live their lives in pain and confusion?

The answer, fortunately, is no. Though Mime could not reforge Siegfried's sword, *Siegfried himself managed to do so*. And in almost all versions of the Grail Legend, Perceval succeeds in getting back to the Grail Castle and healing the Fisher King. But as we shall see, a man's deepest, most spiritual wound can only be healed when he is able to regain his own center of being, to recover his personal sense of heroism by embarking on a road which leads to self-discovery.

But Perceval, at the beginning of the story, is young and still incapable of doing this. He sees the lance dripping blood, the jewel-encrusted chalice, the silver serving tray. He mentally questions the meaning of all these things, even as he wonders over the damsel carrying the grail. But he remains silent. He does not use his voice to project his thoughts, his instinctual feelings of curiosity. Had he done so he might have understood the direction he himself must take in order to make his mark on the world. But his chance escapes him, and in the morning he finds himself alone in the castle; he barely gets out before the drawbridge snaps shut.

Most modern men, like Perceval, have been given a sword, whether they wanted one or not. Clearly we, like Perceval, do not yet know how to use it to heal ourselves or the Fisher King. What do the myths tells us, then, about the path we must take in order to reforge our broken swords and use them with genuine masculine empowerment?

The sword is a weapon of destructive force, used by a Warrior on the field of battle. To wield a sword properly requires the strength brought about by arduous physical training, spiritual aggression, and that heroic courage which grants the bearer the ability to fight against ever-encroaching darkness. The sword is therefore symbolic of purification and spiritual evolution, for the swordsman is often the slayer of dragons—especially inner dragons of his own making. And to raise his courage to the point where he may do battle with his demons, the Warrior must often evoke his "battle frenzy."

This brings us back to Cuchulain, for it is in the fury of battle that Cuchulain becomes truly magical. In fact, he loses most of his purely human attributes and becomes another creature altogether. The old Irish sagas tell us that when Cuchulain goes into his battle frenzy his body is wracked by contortions. He is transformed. He turns right around in his skin so that his feet and his knees face the rear while his calves and buttocks face front. His hair stands up on end and each separate hair glows with fire or with blood. Flames pour out of his mouth and a geyser of thick black blood spurts out of the top of his head. One eye sinks back into his skull while the other protrudes out to his cheek, glowing fiercely. On his forehead appears a sign which the sagas call "the hero's moon." Once Cuchulain has managed to get himself into this fearsome state he is invincible, and one must plunge him into three vats of cold water to cool him down.

Cuchulain in his battle frenzy is not quite human. He has become one with the spirit of destruction. It is this ability which makes him the superb Warrior he is. But many men in our own day and age only get in touch with this part of their inner Warrior when they become violent through frustrated rage. This can cause them to abuse women, get into barroom brawls, or collect guns after the manner of the survivalists. Men in this condition are a bit reminiscent of the Red Knights or Black Knights who haunt the Arthurian legends. The questing knight generally encounters these dark-spirited individuals in the woods, among wild places. The Black Knight or Red Knight has pitched his pavilion near a stream or a crossroads. Here he challenges all comers to battle, though apparently without reason or purpose. Rather than defend fair ladies, he often rapes or beheads them. A gloomy, half feral denizen of the forest, he kills for the simple pleasure of it.

So as we can see, the Warrior can become a liability—in legend as well as in real life—when his rage overcomes him. How, then, does this same ferocious battle-rage make Cuchulain a hero?

Let us remember that Cuchulain was fatherless. Like Perceval in the forest, he grew up in his mother's world. A strong male force, a male power, was notably absent. But Cuchulain wanted to be a Warrior—a quintessentially male path. What did he do?

The child Cuchulain picked up his spear and his hurley stick and walked across the country alone, all the way to the court of Conor mac Nessa. He went to see the King.

Cuchulain sought out his mentor. King Conor mac Nessa was the titular head of the Red Branch, a sacred order of Warriors, of heroes. He was also Cuchulain's uncle, the brother of the child's mother, Dectera. Traditionally we must seek out a mentor among those who have followed the same path we seek to follow: if we aspire to be accountants, we must learn about the art (and the way of life it implies) from an older, wiser accountant. A mentor is not the same as a father. Our fathers are too close to us to play the role of mentor or initiator. For that task, a certain amount of detachment is required, both on the part of the mentor as well as his apprentice. This is because children (especially Warrior children) tend to reject the aspirations held for them by their parents. The father figure and, more specifically, his professional interest, is often rejected in favor of something different, new and definitely more exciting. This could be anything, of course. If the father is an eccentric artist the son might choose to become an actuary; if Dad is vice president of the local bank the Warrior child may rove the world as a hired mercenary. Therefore, in traditional societies, the mentor role is often played by a male relative—like Conor, who was Cuchulain's uncle. Many of us today, however, must seek our mentors outside of the family circle. Sometimes, as Robert Bly points out, we must even seek them outside the circle of the living! Bly himself could find no wise old poets in Minnesota to guide him, so he studied the life of William Butler Yeats, taking that historical figure as his mentor.

Cuchulain was a wise child when he set off alone to seek the King. The rage that could have consumed him, made him into a monster instead of a hero, was channeled under the wise care of Cuchulain's mentor—or perhaps we should say "mentors," for the warriors themselves were trained not by the King personally, but by the champion, Fergus mac Roy. Cuchulain's rage came to serve a purpose. He was fighting for his King.

It is important to note that Conor mac Nessa was more than just a mentor—he was also a *King*. We live in a democratic world, and we have been taught that monarchs are a social evil. We have been taught to define the word "King" in the same terms as "tyrant." The women's movement, too, has often seen fit to regard the archetype of the King as a mere negative vestige of an oppressive patriarchy—in other words, we may too often define King as "patriarchal tyrant." But this is not at all what a King meant to the peoples of ancient Europe.

Although we shall consider the King at more length later on, there are a few points which we must bring up now. Most importantly, the King was regarded as the visible symbol of his people—the soul of the collective embodied in one individual. The capital city or sacred hill (like Tara or Emain Macha in ancient Ireland) was the symbolic center of the universe, the place where the King, archetype of the people, celebrated his ritual marriage with the land itself. Without the King to serve as the central axis or World Tree for the land and the people on it, cosmic balance could not be maintained. Similarly, in astrology, the sun was regarded as the King, and all the other planets subservient to it (and this concept long predates the Copernican model of the universe). Hence the pharaohs of Egypt, the sacred centers or World Trees of the Egyptian people, were incarnations of the sun.

Carrying this astrological model a little further, we may note that the sun is considered, in modern astrology, as a symbol of an individual's vital essence or true inner Self. The sun is the center or core of our being. When Cuchulain "goes to see the King," he is placing his Warrior energies at the disposal of the kingdom's sacred center.

This is another way of saying that we must place our own Warrior spirit at the service of our central core of being, our true selves. *To fight for any force other than our true Self is to pervert the Warrior energy and render it brutal.*

Let us also remember that in astrology the sun is said to be "exalted" (i.e. to reach its highest potential) in the sign of Aries, which is ruled by the planet Mars, the war god. And Mars, the Warrior's planet, is itself exalted in Capricorn, sign of the sun-king who is born at the winter solstice. This tells us that the Warrior can merge his individuality and destiny with his strong motivational skills. The greatest outcome of this interior fusion of will and purpose is the realization that, ultimately, the Warrior has no control over the end result of his actions, but performs his acts of valor and courage for the greater good of the kingdom and its inhabitants rather than for himself alone.

The Black Knight or Red Knight who fights alone at his camp in the forest owes allegiance to no King. He is a lone wolf, a renegade. Like some modern mercenary, he wanders the world in search of a fight—*any* fight. It need not be a fight for his own principles. It is not necessary that his true Self should direct him or choose a cause, a crusade, to make of him a sacred Warrior. He just likes to kill things.

To fight on behalf of the true Self is sometimes a purely personal matter, though usually it implies devotion to some larger cause. A man may do battle in the world of business or politics simply to build for himself a life of success, a sense of security, a social profile he can believe in. More often, however, the ancient mythological kings sent their knights or warriors out to fight for some particular cause—to defend a woman, to rescue a castle, to recover a sacred relic or perform some other altruistic, transpersonal task. Thus the

Warrior was required to cultivate inner qualities which were just as important as his physical strength. Finn MacCool was the leader of a warrior band called the Fiana or Fenians (a name taken up by later Irish revolutionaries who believed themselves to be acting in the spirit of Finn). He and his men protected Ireland against all invaders and and perils. The physical training necessary to become a member of the Fiana was arduous. A candidate had to be buried up to his knees in a pit and, armed only with a shield and a wand of magic hazel, to ward off nine warriors who attacked him with spears. He had to run through the forest, pursued by the other Fenians; not only must he avoid being caught, he must not break a single branch in the forest. Beyond that, he had to leap over a branch as high as his forehead and stoop beneath one as low as his knee. In addition to these physical requirements, there were the ethical ones: a Fenian had to renounce his clan or family and dedicate his energies to the brotherhood, he had to be a bard as well as a fighter, he could never refuse hospitality to anyone, never turn his back in battle, and never be cruel or insulting to women.

The code of the Fenians clearly differs in many respects from the belief system of today's "macho man." How many gang members, barroom brawlers, beat cops, soldiers, boxers, sports fans, and late-night wrestling enthusiasts admit to reading or composing poetry, or tracking the patterns of history (another bardic activity) in their off hours? Machismo is a strange and wondrous phenomenon, for those who cling to its credo ("be rude, be crude, be a tough dude") are absolved from life's more refined responsibilities and from manifesting ex-President Bush's "kinder, gentler nation" where it rightfully belongs—within.

One of the secrets involved with being a Warrior is this: there is *power* in helplessness, in recognizing one's vulnerabilities, frailties, and limitations. Only when the Warrior reaches inward to do battle with the darkness of his own shadow can he begin to assess the weaknesses of his true enemy. The Warrior needs to hone his mental and emotional faculties as well as his physical body if he is to survive in the chess game of life.

The mass of humanity is transported along, controlled by and resigned to its immediate environment, the will and desires of others, genetics, heredity, suggestion, and a host of outward causes. The genuine Sacred Warrior is a master who rises above his lower and more instinctual urges. He is able to control his mood, character, quality, and power as well as his external environment. He becomes the man who makes the moves, not the pawn in the game. He is a player, rather than one who is maneuvered by other wills and circumstances. He understands that he must make use of the principle of cause and effect rather than being its tool. His obedience is to his inner King, a force greater than his personal self. But the Warrior is the master of his own level of existence. And he must *know his levels* if he is to fight and to win.

And the final result of all his battles? The Warrior may grow into a King. He may win a kingdom by virtue of his heroism. This is another way of saying that if the Warrior fights for his true Self long enough, he will become one with that Self. It is perhaps one of the great tragedies of our times that the veterans of Vietnam, fighting for a cause deemed unworthy by so many, rejected as losers or butchers upon their return home, were seldom given the opportunity to grow into Kings like the World War II veterans before them. Too many have remained Red Knights, lost in spirit, riding through dark forests in search of another battle.

A man becomes a true hero or Sacred Warrior when he fights for a cause. But what cause? Can it be *any* cause? We are entering a strange, gray area here, are we not? If a given individual protests against war while his brother flies jets in Iraq, are both of them Sacred Warriors? Or is one cause preferable to the other? Fight for Greenpeace or campaign for the Republicans? For or against abortion? How shall we distinguish the high-spirited Warrior upon a quest from the fanatic? Neither one is precisely the same kind of "lone wolf" as is the Black or Red Knight. Both are fighting for a cause they consider transpersonal, greater than themselves. And yet some of these crusaders lose all sense of fairness, of generosity, of spirit. What is the difference?

The difference, of course, is that we must be aware of our true Self, must know what it needs and wants, the melody that makes it sing, before we can rightly choose our cause. And sometimes the Self is difficult to find. Sometimes we must go through initiation in order to discover it. And according to Celtic myth, the Warrior is often initiated through channels which we may find quite unexpected: both Finn MacCool and Cuchulain were initiated into the arts of war by women. Even the unfortunate Sir Balin gained his sword from a woman—and for that matter, so did King Arthur, who received Excalibur from the Lady of the Lake.

Finn MacCool, like most of our Celtic heroes, suffered from the lack of a father, for his own sire was slain in battle even before Finn's birth. In order to protect him from the wrath of the father's enemies, the boy was taken from his mother and raised in the forest (again like Perceval) by two women identified as Bodball the Druidess and "the Gray One of Luachar." Elsewhere in the old saga, Finn's rescuers are called "the two warrior-women."[10]

Cuchulain is an even more specific case in point. The hero of Ulster was sent to the Isle of Skye to become perfected in the arts of war, and there his teacher was one Scathach (also spelled Skya after the island where she made her home). And lest we imagine that these Warrior Women were training the old heroes in arts esoteric or erotic, the story of Cuchulain is quite explicit about the fact that Scathach was teaching him to *fight*.[11]

All of this makes for a rather different scenario than the one projected by most writers on male myths. We have been told, in fact, that a man *cannot* be initiated by women and that, in order to understand the parameters involved with being a man, he must be initiated by other men.[12] But, in view of the myths which lie before us, we must make a more subtle distinction: parameters may indeed determine the specific *form* of a function, but they do not define the *interior nature* of that function. The internal dimensions of any male archetype can only be fully realized by developing a relationship with the anima, the "lady soul" within.

The female figure in men's myths most often signifies the anima, which is to say the soul. So it is the soul—perhaps in the person of a real woman—which initiates a man, even the isolated Warrior, who must draw his courage and his sense of purpose from the soul. For really effective work in any field, both the male and female polarities must be activated. This is even true for the Warrior and King, the most thoroughly masculine of archetypes. So we should not be surprised to find that an Amazon sleeps within the soul of the male Warrior, a "lady soul" to match his own power and courage.

The Warrior's potential relationship with the anima or Amazon within may bring him hope; it provides the light at the end of the tunnel that can guide him out of the encroaching darkness. The Warrior seldom finds his way out of the dark all alone. To fight his way out of the loneliness, the Warrior must enter into relationship with something—or, more to the point, with some*one*. He must awaken his own inner Lover, for as we shall see, there is a Lover in every Warrior's soul.

But before we move on to the next Grail Treasure, the next male archetype, it is time that we paused to assess the Warrior spirit within ourselves. Because of the various directions we take during our childhood, we tend to be a combination of each of the four male archetypes. Almost no one is a "pure" type. But an archetype may be either mature or immature, and in a society which has lost touch with the empowerment of those archetypes there is a tendency for the immature side of the myth to take control. Problems arise when we allow this immature child-self to rule our adult selves, problems which become ever more frustrating as the Wheel of the Seasons spins and urges us toward transcendence—a goal which is not in the interests of the grumpy child within. It is never easy to recognize or change our habitual negative behavior patterns. It is never easy to travel the Wheel all the way round and become caring, concerned, mature human beings. More often than not, we may find it "safer" to take the path of least resistance and live out our lives as ultimate couch potatoes. But it is also true that this seldom works for us. Evolution is part and parcel of the ever-present constancy of change. We have no choice but to keep on moving.

Where, then, do we stand on the Wheel of the Seasons, and at what station upon the turrets of the Revolving Castle? Which of the Four Grail Treasures, brought to us from the world of the gods by the Tuatha de Danaan, has flowered most fully within us? And is it flowering or blighted?

Some guidelines will follow each of the chapters on the four male archetypes. We hope that it will assist you in the process of self-definition.

Cuchulain Receives Instruction from the Warrior Woman Skya

Your inner Warrior expresses itself positively if:

1. You take a dramatic, self-confident stance in life.

2. You admire and emulate sports figures, heroes, or avenging angels.

3. You volunteered to join the armed forces during wartime because you genuinely wanted to protect those near to you and serve a higher cause.

4. You are protective of others, a "knight in shining armor," willing to come to the aid of the helpless, weak, and oppressed.

5. You use reason prior to action.

6. You are brave, bold, and assertive.

7. You are extraverted, public, political, and determined.

8. You are responsible, proud, honorable, and self-respecting.

9. You prefer the wild, free abandon of the hunt, the office, or the car phone to the familiar domestic duties demanded of you on the home front.

10. You are in control of your temper and not afraid to express sadness and grief.

Your inner Warrior expresses itself negatively if:

1. You idolize tough guys, criminals, or warmongers, or act the part of bully, show-off, or coward.

2. You engage in power plays typically involving love-hate relationships, exaggerated loyalties and cruelty, courage and cowardice.

3. You blame others for your shortcomings.

4. You attempt to establish a pecking order or hierarchy in which you are the final authority figure.

5. You believe that "might makes right" and advocate a "my way or the highway" attitude towards the world.

6. You build up your body solely for the sake of self-defense or to prove that you are powerful and can engage in or endure violence.

7. You are combative, argumentative, and a champion of verbal warfare.

8. You limit your view of life to pairs of opposites such as black and white, right and wrong, good and evil.

9. You are paranoid, trusting others only when allies are required to assist you in battling a common enemy.

10. You often feel anger, but deny your sadness and tears as being too "feminine."

Notes

1. Don Henley and Glenn Frey, "Desperado" (Los Angeles: Asylum Records, Kicking Bear/Benchmark Music [ASCAP], 1973).

2. Sam Keen, *Fire in the Belly: On Being a Man* (New York: Bantam Books, 1992).

3. Moore and Gillette, *King, Warrior, Magician, Lover*, 75–96.

4. Jeffrey Gantz, trans., *The Mabinogion* (London: Penguin, 1976), 97–117.

5. Robert Graves, *The White Goddess* (New York: Farrar, Straus and Giroux, 1974), 27–60.

6. "The Spoils of Annwn," quoted in Charles Squire, *Celtic Myth and Legend, Poetry and Romance* (Van Nuys, CA: Newcastle Publishing Co., 1975), 319–20.

7. Squire, *Celtic Myth and Legend*, 316–7.

8. Mircea Eliade, *Shamanism: Archaic Techniques of Ecstasy* (Princeton: Princeton-Bollingen, 1974), 62–4.

9. Sir Thomas Malory, *Le Morte D'Arthur* (New York: Mentor, 1962), 43–56. See also the beautiful analysis of this tale in Heinrich Zimmer, *The King and the Corpse* (Princeton: Princeton-Bollingen, 1973), 136–49.

10. Cross, Tom Peete, and Clark Harris Slover, eds., *Ancient Irish Tales* (New York: Barnes and Noble, 1969), 361.

11. McCana, *Celtic Mythology*, 86.

12. Robert Bly, *Iron John: A Book About Men* (Reading, MS: Addison-Wesley Publishing Co., 1990), 16–7.

CHAPTER 3

The Lover

The narrative poem entitled *Sir Gawain and the Green Knight*[1] was written near the end of the Middle Ages (c. 1375), in an England which was predominantly Christian and Anglo-Saxon. The poem's meter thumps along like the tromping of so many Saxon boots. But that relentless thud nevertheless carries us into the mist-haunted world of Celtic paganism, and delimits the dreamy terrain common to both the Warrior and the Lover.

The poem's narrative begins on Christmas Day, when Arthur is holding court at Camelot. Into the celebration rides the most peculiar knight anyone has ever seen, for he is gigantic in size and his hair, his face, and his clothing—even his horse—are all green. His green beard and hair are long, wild, and unruly, and his only weapons are an axe and a staff of holly.

The Green Knight asks that some member of Arthur's court strike him a blow with the axe. Sir Gawain answers the challenge and slices off the green man's head. But the spectral knight simply rises and picks up his own head, which delivers a speech to the assembled company, calling upon Gawain to meet him at the Green Chapel on New Year's Day, a year hence, and to receive a similar blow in return.

Gawain rides forth in the winter of the next year, a pentagram upon his chest (most peculiar in a medieval Christian poem). Like the Warrior, he rides alone, the questing knight in the wilderness. He rides through the rain and the snow and the muck until he comes to a mysterious castle—not unlike the Grail Castle. Here Gawain is entertained royally by the lord of the castle. He is introduced to the lord's beautiful wife and to an aged crone. He is told that the Green Chapel is not far off and that his quest may thus be fulfilled.

Meanwhile, however, there are three days to wait until Gawain's fateful rendezvous with the green man. As he lingers in the castle, the lord rides out every day to hunt. The master's beautiful wife approaches Gawain three times. Three times she attempts to seduce him, and three times he refuses, out of respect for the lord of the castle. Finally, though, he accepts her token—a garter of green.

When Gawain at last rides forth upon New Year's Day, he discovers that the Green Chapel is in fact a prehistoric barrow mound. He stands upon the fairy mound; the Green Knight descends from the cliffs. Gawain kneels as the Green Knight lifts his axe. But the axe only nicks Sir Gawain, and then the Green Knight declares the contest at an end. He reveals that it has all been a test, and that he himself is the lord of the castle in disguise. The test has been devised by the enchantress Morgan Le Fay, the ancient crone Gawain met upon his arrival at the castle.

Sir Gawain and the Green Knight contains the survival of a most ancient ritual,[2] but one which, in this poem at least, has been confused by the Christian monk who authored the poem. It marks the path of a Warrior who, by becoming the champion of the Goddess, also becomes a Lover.

This process in the soul is delineated more clearly in the *Mabinogion*, which retains more of the archaic character of pagan myth. The "First Branch" of this Welsh collection of stories concerns Pwyll, Prince of Dyfed.[3] As he is hunting in the woods, he is confronted by a ghostly figure who runs with a pack of magic

Champion of the Goddess

hounds—none other than Arawn, King of Annwn, a Welsh name for the Celtic Otherworld. Arawn begs a boon of Pwyll: the Prince of Dyfed must descend to the Underworld, there to do battle with Havgan, an opponent whom Arawn has so far failed to slay. As a reward, Pwyll may enjoy Arawn's lady, the Underworld queen.

Pwyll, however, refuses the lady's favor—and for the same reason as Gawain, because of his respect for her lord. Pwyll turns his face to the wall and leaves the queen wondering. But he fulfills his duty and slays Havgan, the mystic warrior whose name means "summer-white."

Herein lies a clue to the ancient ritual. The Green Knight, who appears at the winter solstice carrying a club of Yuletide holly, has all the symbolism of the wintertime, while Havgan is clearly associated with the summer. It was Sir James Frazer, in his famous work *The Golden Bough*,[4] who first enunciated the now-famous theory of the annual combat for the Goddess. In the most ancient times, he argues, a young man was chosen to be the consort (both son and lover) of the Great Goddess. He ritually slew the Goddess's old consort. The aging consort symbolized winter, while the young hero signified summer. The battle between the two men, both lovers of the Goddess, symbolized the Wheel of the Year, ever turning, from summer to winter and back again at the time of the solstices. The young god (Gawain) triumphed like the summer sun, grew hot, then old, then died at the winter solstice. A new lord, like Pwyll, who championed the goddess of earth in her winter sleep, now reigned—until the next solstice, when the new young harvest god, lord of the sunlight, arose to slay him in his turn.

Men go forth to do battle for the Goddess—as Gawain unknowingly went into battle with the young Goddess's green token and at the behest of the goddess-as-crone, Morgan le Fay. They win her in the heat of their young passion, then they grow old. In time, they may be displaced. But the Goddess goes on and on. Ever changing, she is ever changeless.

In ancient times, there was no need for an archetype such as the Lover. All men, in their turn, became the consort of the Goddess; as such, they were Lover and Warrior all in one, like Pwyll or Gawain. Then, in time, they laid down the mantle of the Lover-Son and took up their position as elders, as Kings and Magicians. But we live in a different world. We are fascinated by the Goddess in all her manifestations, and many men worship her to the exclusion of all else. Woman has become the great prize, the eternal treasure to be won. Woman, almost, is the Grail itself! And indeed, in one sense the Grail may be said to symbolize, for men, the Goddess who lies within them.

The Tarot suit of Cups corresponds to the suit of Hearts in modern playing cards and indicates love, merriment, joy, gladness, and delight. It symbolizes the element of water, associated with wisdom, memory, and receptivity. Cups express our sense of well-being, profundity, and beauty, and hence represent the emotional rather than the mental plane.

In its most transcendent form, the cup is the chalice or grail which holds wine or blood. Thus it contains a fluidic substance which, in Hindu philosophy, is called *prakriti*, the cosmic mind-stuff or, to use a Celtic term, the "water of life." We may also think of the chalice visually as two halves of a sphere placed back to back, symbolizing receptivity to spiritual forces as well as protection of and from earthly energies. If this visual image were placed on its side, we would behold the waxing and waning moon.

Though the moon is usually associated with silver and the chalice in our story is made of gold, there is no real question that moon and chalice both represent the divine feminine. This feminine component of reality is notoriously changeable; the moon is a shape-shifter due to its constant cycle of growth and decay. Mediating, receptive, imaginative, and protective as well as dangerous, the moon has long been associated with magic. Looking back at Perceval's initial experience in the Grail Castle, we may guess that the presence of the chalice indicates that Perceval has most certainly entered the Otherworld—and possibly the netherworld as well. Either way, the grail gives us a hint that Perceval may be brought face to face with unpredictable circumstances which will threaten his sense of security when he is least prepared to defend himself.

As we have noted, the mythological Celtic original of the grail was the Cauldron of the Dagda, sometimes called the Cauldron of the Goddess or simply the Cauldron of Rebirth. On the psychological level, we may think of "rebirth" in terms of transmutation and growth. In Celtic myth, these cauldrons are sometimes to be discovered underneath the sea or at the bottom of a lake. This is another way of saying that the transformative power of feeling is hidden deep in the unconscious, as well as suggesting a synthesis of the cauldron and that which it contains—the sublimation of instinct which results in the purification of the feeling nature. The cauldron is the grail or chalice in its most primordial form—the grail itself, more consciously exalted, is gold and encrusted with jewels.

In order to achieve the grail, Perceval will have to descend into the deep waters of his unconscious in order to explore and eventually retrieve his own feelings and desires. This is likely to be an earth-shattering experience for Perceval—as it is for most men. In mythology, few men descend easily into the psychic underworld of their own feelings. Orpheus and Theseus both failed in this primal task, though Dionysus—himself more androgynous than purely masculine—managed to succeed.

For most men, as for so many mythological heroes, this descent into the realm of feeling, the realm of the Goddess, is very difficult. First we encounter the Goddess herself, as a tremendous inner figure symbolic of our own inner feminine nature. It is her business to conduct us to those deep levels of the soul which the Celts imaged as the Otherworld (and where, in the course of this book, we shall eventually travel). But the woman within is a stormy guide for most of us to follow. In the first place, we may find it difficult to see her as an inner figure. Rather, we may tend to see her image in the eyes of real women whom we encounter in real life. This casts a man into the deep waters of a great ecstasy which we call romantic love. This is what makes a man the Lover.

Romantic love is one of the most powerful forces affecting the Western psyche. In Eastern cultures, love is expressed through stability, devotion, and loyalty to the cause of daily existence (what the Greeks would have called *caritas* or "loving-kindness" and the early Christians *agape* or spiritual love). But our brand of "true love" here in the West is comprised of an idealistic package of romantic beliefs, attitudes, and expectations welling up from the depths of our souls. Thus we are often blindly dominated by our instinctual reactions

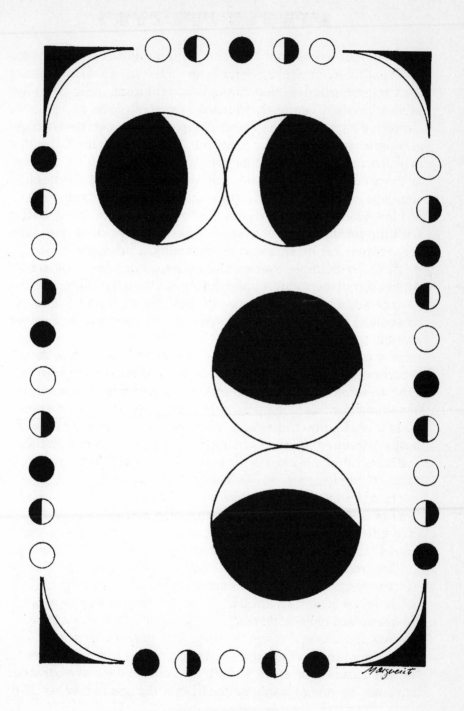

The Lunar Chalice

and inherent primordial behavior patterns when seeking out a potential life-mate. Thus we make the mistake of looking for our own self-reflection in and through a significant other. Thus we become a society genuinely addicted to romantic love.

As we have seen, the archaic relationship between the Goddess and her champion did not require a figure such as the Lover, the man enamored of the feminine principle. This archetype appears to have surfaced somewhat later, and when an archetype comes into consciousness it usually does so in a tempestuous and troubled fashion. Hence many stories of the Lover in old Celtic myth deal with the *problem* of the Lover, or what can happen to men who become too deeply entranced by the feminine principle.

Take, for example, the case of Angus mac Og.[5] His name means Angus, son of the Young, or perhaps Angus the Ever-Young. He was one of the most popular of the old Irish deities; rural Irish people reverenced him as one of the leaders of the fairy folk on into the nineteenth century. His home or "hill" *(sidhe)* was the great megalithic tomb of Newgrange. It was here, presumably, that Angus experienced his vision or "dream." A beautiful maiden, shining with light, appeared to him as he slept. Upon awakening, he could think of nothing else. He took up the search for his magic maiden, casting aside all his godly duties and prerogatives, wandering aimlessly, intent only upon "her." His quest lasted for many mortal lifetimes, and is beautifully evoked in the poem by William Butler Yeats:

> *Though I am old with wandering*
> *Through hollow lands and hilly lands,*
> *I will find out where she has gone,*
> *And kiss her lips and take her hands;*
> *And walk among long dappled grass,*
> *And pluck till time and times are done*
> *The silver apples of the moon,*
> *The golden apples of the sun.*[6]

In time, Angus discovered that his love was a swan maiden; he himself became a swan, dove with her beneath the waves, and has ever after been known among the Irish as the god of love.

Pwyll, the Welsh hero who fought for the Goddess in the Otherworld, later encountered her on earth as well. She appeared to him one night as he slept a magical sleep atop an ancient barrow mound. He beheld her riding a horse through the moonlight, her long hair blowing behind her and her whole being shining with an Otherworldly glow. Night after night he pursued her, but her elvish steed always stayed just ahead of him, beyond his reach. At last he stopped pursuing her and approached her with knightly courtesy. And so he won her and made her his wife. Her name was Rhiannon.

But what about those of us who are not mythic heroes or gods? What is our response to the vision, the appearance of the glorious Goddess who comes to us, most often, in the shape of a mortal woman—a woman seen through the eyes of ecstasy and fantasy, a woman made unreal by our dreams? Can we nurture and protect that shining vision which keeps her Otherworldly, inhuman? Can we prevent her from falling off her pedestal, becoming once again a mere mortal with likes and dislikes, good habits and bad? Can we leave the world behind and dive with her beneath the waves, there to dwell like two magical swans for all time?

We cannot. We are human—and so, ultimately, is she, no matter how gloriously may shine the robes of the Goddess when first we set eyes upon her. This problem—which Jungian psychologists call the "anima problem"—appears first in such ancient myths as that of Angus, or in the story of Dermot and Grania.[7] Dermot O'Dyna was one of the companions of Finn MacCool. Old Finn took a young bride named Grania, and that's where the trouble began. Grania fell in love with Dermot and called upon him to be her champion. He ran away with her and spent years in the forest with his beloved, pursued by Finn and by the men who had once been his companions.

This story of Dermot and Grania arose again with great power in the twelfth century, when it took shape in the Arthurian romances. That upheaval marked a new epoch in the consciousness of Western man. No longer was he united with the earth and the Great Goddess in the ancient round of birth, death, and rebirth that we have seen imaged in the tales of Pwyll and Gawain. The Goddess had slipped into the unconscious of European humanity, only to emerge as a glimmering, mystical figure, clothed in a radiance which was both spiritual and erotic. Though one may find tales of erotic passion in the legends of Greece and Rome, one will search in vain for instances of "falling in love" as we now understand the term. That began with the twelfth century romances and the poems of the Troubadours, and we have never been the same since. The Lover had emerged into our collective consciousness.[8]

We may trace the progress of the Lover through our more recent history as well. Troubadours came into full swing again in the 1940s with Frank Sinatra at stage center. Suave, fashionable, and debonair, Old Blue Eyes crooned to enamored audiences and initiated them into the cult of Love Italian-style. But that was merely the first blow to our society's Puritanical mores; the real explosion emerged in the 1950s, when we made the auditory and visual transition to Elvis Presley and became entranced with his gyrating pelvis and his little-boy-lost brand of back-country rock. The English invasion came next; Americans were captured by four mop-headed boys who called themselves the Beatles. And while they played rock-and-roll with charming and whimsical abandon to hordes of frenzied prepubescent teeny-boppers, grown women began making undergarment offerings to Welsh pop singer Tom Jones.

The tides of change had silently converged upon the mind-set of Western civilization. Throughout the 1960s, a sexual revolution of "free love" became the prevalent theme, signifying the emergence of ecstatic archetypes like Dionysus into the mainstream of American culture. Perhaps the most Dionysiac of all these contemporary Lover archetypes was Jim Morrison. Calling himself the Lizard King—as if to symbolize the dark and brooding fertility of the netherworld—Morrison went beyond all social mores to elicit sexual excitation from his fans and followers. A heightened—and thus intrinsically spiritual—approach toward what many regarded as wild, unbridled promiscuity satisfied our collective inclination toward alternative spiritual practices. (It may also have fostered a fair amount of accelerated personal transformation.)

By the end of the 60s, we were well on the way to embracing Peter Pan as our predominant national archetype. No one wanted to grow up. We lost interest in taking responsibility for our actions or committing ourselves to long-term relationships. The "swinging single" predominated in the dating game and divorce escalated among the married. We only cooled our quest for romantic perfection after 1977 and the beginning of the AIDS epidemic. Traditional concepts of home and family have once more begun to influence our search for the perfect mate.

The "perils of the soul" inherent in such a search for continuous romantic ecstasy were well known to the first great romantics of Western culture, the Troubadours and courtly poets. Of all the tales of knights and their ladies which follow the outlines of the Dermot and Grania story, the most powerful and mythically charged is also one of the earliest. This is the tale of Tristan and Iseult.[9]

Tristan is a knight in the court of Mark, King of Cornwall. He is sent to Ireland to acquire a bride for the king—the princess Iseult, daughter of a sorceress. Iseult loathes Tristan, who has slain one of her relatives in knightly combat. The voyage back to Cornwall is charged with animosity—so deeply charged, in fact, that Iseult resolves to die rather than join with her enemies. She calls upon her maid Branwen to pour a cup of the poison her sorceress mother had mixed for her in case of dire emergency. Then she calls upon Tristan to drink with her. But Branwen, who loves her mistress, cannot bear to see her die, and fills the cup with a love potion rather than with poison. Tristan and Iseult fall in love. In time, King Mark learns of their passion for each other and they are forced to flee, like Dermot and Grania, to the woods. There they live in wilderness rapture in a lovers' grotto. But in time they are discovered and forced to flee again. Their lives become a flight from the past, so that the passion which gives them life also, in time, wears them down and brings them to their deaths.

A man who gives himself up utterly to love—who, to put it another way, becomes possessed by the Lover archetype—undergoes a mystical experience. In the eyes of his beloved, he beholds the Goddess herself. His world revolves around her. His mystical rapture is in many ways equivalent to death—for as we have seen, the cup administered by Branwen (who also appears in the *Mabinogion* as a sorrowing Persephone but who was in ancient times worshiped in Cornwall as the goddess of love) was supposed to contain poison rather than nectar. The two cannot be separated. To experience mystical bliss is to drink of the nectar of the gods, indeed; but it is also to die, at least to ordinary human concerns, as Hindu yogis and Hermetic mystics customarily spoke of dying to "the world" when they entered upon a spiritual path.

But when a man renounces his consciousness of self to worship the Goddess, he enters very treacherous waters—after all, Iseult was the daughter of a sorceress! In Celtic tradition, it is almost always the Warrior who takes up the chalice of the Lover. And when he does so, he inevitably offends against his King—as Dermot offended Finn, Tristan Mark, or Lancelot Arthur. He has ceased to battle for the sake of the Self, the inner sun or inner King. A man who is under the Lover's spell no longer places his courage and prowess at the service of his inner directive force. By so doing, he has ceased to be a Warrior at all. Now he is a Lover, which is an entirely different animal.

But, you may say, why is this necessarily a problem? The Goddess, in ancient times, had her champions like Pwyll and Gawain. Why should she not have them still?

The problem arises when a man seeks the Goddess in mortal women. When a man falls madly in love—with his Midwestern Grania, his secretarial Guinevere, his high school Iseult—he isn't really in love with *her*. In fact, he may know nothing about her— who she really is, her likes and dislikes, strengths and weaknesses. He is simply worshipping the Goddess—and the Goddess, as we all know, lies *within him*. He has taken up the search for perfection in the all-too-human realm of personal relationships. The object of his love and devotion becomes a mirror image of the qualities he would most like to claim for himself. But these are qualities which, for some reason, the Lover believes he lacks. Or perhaps he simply has no wish to take responsibility for the hard work of developing these personality traits.

What, then, occurs when we project our unconscious longings onto another? Often, the result is a "gaslight" effect. As the ancient philosophy of polarities suggests, like attracts like. Looking into love's magic mirror, the eyes of our beloved partner, we eventually come to see a mirror image opposite—all our own weaknesses, the frailties and negative patterns which impelled us to seek perfection through another in the first place!

Thus, in time, a man is bound to discover that his Iseult, his magical sorceress, is simply a human being. And if he is a wise and mature man, he will learn to deal with her and love her as a human being. But if he is more passionate than wise, more inspired than sensible, he will drop her like a hot potato and run off in search of yet another Goddess. This creates the character type which Jungian analysts call the *puer aeternus* or eternal child[10]—pop psychology calls him a Peter Pan, with equal justification. He cannot abandon his attachment to the Goddess of Love. Therefore he never quite grows up. Smiling, charming, handsome, and debonair, he dances from one Goddess to the other—eternally in love, eternally suffering the disappointments of reality, and eternally trying again.

This problem Lover may be a very talented fellow. After all, he has tasted of the Goddess's chalice; he has sipped the mead of inspiration. He may be a poet, painter, or musician of great gifts— but so long as he spends his life seeking the Goddess in the eyes of mortal women, he is unlikely ever to settle down and acquire the Warrior spirit necessary to bring his talents to fruition. As we have seen, he who would *create* must wield the sword.

Perceval's Grail Castle experience suggested that he needed to dive deep into the waters of the unconscious in order to find the true cauldron of rebirth. And similarly, the Lover must dive deep into his own unconscious in order to discover that the Goddess lives within, in his own Otherworld. Only by so doing can he break the habit of *projecting* her power onto mortal women, and thus reclaim her as an inner figure, his own anima, the inspirer of his poetry, his art, or simply his sense of universal love and compassion.

To bring forth the anima from his inner depths is a difficult and perilous task for a man to undertake. For a Lover, it constitutes the heroic journey par excellence. Consider the case of Sir Gawain (whose adventures, by the way, contain more true pagan myth than those of any of the other Arthurian knights, persuading some scholars to believe that Gawain himself is surely an ancient god in medieval disguise). While questing for the Holy Grail, Gawain sailed in a boat to a small island in the midst of an enchanted lake.

Here he encountered a castle inhabited only by women. This Castle of Damsels was under an enchantment, a spell which it was up to Gawain to remove. But his first thought was simply to get a good rest. The damsels led him to a bedchamber—but as soon as he lay down, the bed began to shake, rumble, and finally to fly madly about the room. Then a raging lion attacked the knight.

Gawain prevailed over both the runaway bed and the raging lion; he released the Castle of Damsels from its enchantment and became lord of the cxastle. At this point, however, different versions of the story take widely divergent paths. Some versions say that Gawain continued his quest—in other words, he had mastered the power of his own anima and was able to return to the world and to act effectively there. (In a more mystical or esoteric context, the raging lion may signify here, as it does in alchemy and the Tarot, the yogic control of the kundalini or feminine power itself.) But other versions of the story imply that Gawain remained in the castle as its lord—in other words, he remained rapt in contemplation of his own unconscious, of the woman within him, never to return to the world at large and continue his destiny as a knight. Even after wrestling to bring forth the anima, a man may still be under her spell.[11]

The divine feminine represents to man that part of himself over which he seems to have no control. However, there is an integral relationship between masculine and feminine energy, a unity of mind and heart which can only be attained by mastering one's instincts and desires. Unless he can overcome his unwanted responses and replace them with habit patterns which are free of fear and self-condemnation, a man cannot become a fully conscious being. He cannot stand at the center of the Grail Castle and exercise the creative expression of his own individual selfhood. The ability to control his emotions—the feeling-substance which fills the chalice of the Goddess—enables a man to share his affections from the heart. This does not mean that he gives up his masculine identity. He may continue to protect, provide, hunt, fish, and even open car doors for women who still appreciate it. He need not become lost in the realm of the Goddess simply because he has dared to get in touch with his feminine nature.

Why, then, do so many of us, like Gawain, fail to find our way back from the Castle of Damsels? Perhaps because most of us are still primarily motivated by instinct, by subjective feelings rather than objective reasoning. Like the tragic Balin, we carry swords which lie under the spell of a feminine enchantment and cannot function with the pure discriminative power which myth demands of them. This is especially true today, in a world of "soft" men initiated primarily into feminine values. And it is this feminine realm of feeling and instinct which is often operative in men's relationships with women.

Our instinct, our basic animal drives, lie behind our submerged habits and responses to others. We ride the mysterious horse of Rhiannon rather than the knight's charger. And if we ourselves are motivated by unconscious patterns and responses, it stands to reason that our marriage partners or mates will share a similar mechanism of automatic or unconscious responses. Romantic bonding—the result of our natural actions and responses—may prevail in the early stages of a relationship, while we are still in the throes of romantic love. But these idyllic circumstances wear thin when our more negative instincts begin to manifest and are projected onto the partner. This is a process that occurs in that part of ourselves we may call the "primordial brain."

This ancient, instinctual component of the brain is part and parcel of our memory banks. It is tied to both the collective and the personal unconscious, representing our survival instincts and our early childhood conditioning. It gives birth to our free-floating fears and anxieties. It also governs the inner responses which draw us into whirlwind courtships and romantic entanglements: over-esteem or under-esteem, poor boundaries, immaturity, extremism, lack of self-care and, in general, the lack of a center. From this primordial stew is born the "soft male" in a man's soul, for the soft male takes the path of least resistance, which is always the unconscious path. In a woman's soul, the corresponding process signals the emergence of the sinister but compelling animus figure called the Dark Lover, who acts as the proverbial backdoor man, spawning chaos in terms of the woman's intimate, emotional expression.

This entire drama takes place in the Fourth Branch of the *Mabinogion*.[12] Lleu Llaw Gyffes got his name, Lleu of the Skillful Hand, because he was the master of many crafts. His mother Arianrhod, Lady of the Silver Wheel, had been forced into giving birth to him; angrily, she put a curse upon him so that he could never lie with any mortal woman. Knowing that the time had come for Lleu to take a wife, the great magician Gwydion ap Don (who was apparently Lleu's father in the original story, though his role is somewhat obscured in the medieval version which survives) went to the high king, Math the Ancient. The two locked themselves away in a chamber and, through magic and enchantment, conjured up a woman made from the flowers of oak and broom and meadowsweet. She had no mortal soul. She was beautiful but vacuous. They called her Blodeuedd, meaning "flower-face," and presented her to Lleu, who immediately fell in love with her and married her. He then set up a court of his own in a place called Mur Castell.

One day Lleu went off to visit Math. Blodeuedd was sitting at home when she heard a horn blow and saw an exhausted stag pursued by dogs, hunters, and men on foot. She sent a servant to inquire as to who these men served, and received the answer, "Goronwy the Staunch, lord of Penllyn." According to the rules of hospitality, she invited Goronwy and his retinue to spend the night at Mur Castell. She was instantly struck by the blood lust running through Goronwy's veins, and he was equally smitten with her fair and delicate beauty. They fell madly in love and slept together that very night. Before Goronwy left Mur Castell, he and Blodeuedd had initiated a plot to kill Lleu.

Lleu may have been skillful; and we know from his Irish counterpart, Lugh, that he was once worshiped as a warrior god. The Irish god Lugh was called the Samildanach, "the man of many gifts," but in this Welsh story his "gifts" of innocence, sensitivity, and naiveté occupy center stage. Goronwy could not have known that Lleu could only be slain through a set of magical circumstances—"neither indoors nor out of doors, neither on horse nor on foot." But Lleu, blinded by his love for the emotionally insubstantial Blodeuedd, told her the secret way by which those magical circumstances could be realized. And because the maid of flowers possessed no will of her own and was drawn to the greatest source of power, she told Goronwy how to kill her husband.

Lleu had put his inner Warrior aside in order to enter the love madness. He became the Lover hidden inside every fighting man. The need to rescue, nurture, protect and defend another is but an outward reflection of one's own deep, innermost desire to be rescued, nurtured, protected and defended. Lleu was not thinking. Like Balin, he declined to wield his sword of discrimination. He was not protecting *himself*. He gave up his own empowerment for love, and thereby allowed his soul to be seized by the perfidy and deceit of another.

> *The silver-wheel moonshadows*
> *Drew him, drowned him.*
> *He was stricken, rendered lost,*
> *Faery spelled. She draped him*
> *With her misty veils.*[13]

If we were to subject the heroes of myth to the regimen of psychoanalysis, we might conclude that Lleu never got over the curse placed upon him by his mother. Instead, he unconsciously transferred his feelings about Arianrhod to his wife Blodeuedd. Perhaps he projected his own invisible rage onto her, and she, the reflecting mirror, sought out Goronwy's more visible rage.

Goronwy is the Dark Lover of women's dreams. He slips into Lleu's castle, sleeps with Lleu's wife, and then plots Lleu's death in order to take all his holdings as well. Here is a sinister figure indeed, a Warrior completely out of touch with his inner feminine. Unlike the soft male who wears his tenderness and sensitivity on his sleeve, the Dark Lover is unconscious of his own fragility. He is afraid of the darkness which will seize him at the moment of his own death. He cannot deal with emotions and is therefore secretly passive or submissive. He is arrogant, prideful, afraid of losing control. He has caught the projection of Blodeuedd's shadow animus, the dark side of the unconscious male figure sleeping within the flower maiden.

Blodeuedd, in turn, is the mirror of Goronwy's unconscious. Her fierce resolve in plotting Lleu's death shows us that she is inwardly strong, yet as the seemingly gentle flower girl she is clearly terrified of her own power. Her attention is focused upon sensation, the logic of the heart, while her actual thoughts are turbulent and undisciplined. Submissive and obedient on the surface, she is manipulative and cruel underneath. She sees herself as a victim and consequently lacks self-identity.

When such a woman finds the Dark Lover—whether within herself or in the form of a man—she discovers aspects of her own inner being. These hidden places in the psyche may lead her to a world of darkness or of light. They led Blodeuedd back into the shadowy realm of the animal totem, for after Lleu was finally speared by Goronwy, Gwydion turned her into an owl. But then, she had never been truly human to begin with.

She may have been made of flowers, but Blodeuedd was not just an empty-headed female. Some flowers are poisonous when eaten, and roses have thorns. Lleu might just as well have been made of flowers himself, for he was in love with an *image* of love, his own inner woman projected upon Blodeuedd. He couldn't see her as having needs and desires of her own. She had been created for him, to be whatever he wanted her to be—and this, of course, is how we are likely to feel about the object of our passion whenever we "fall" in love. Is it any wonder that Blodeuedd betrayed Lleu? Is it any wonder that we feel betrayed when our own "women of flowers" turn out to be someone different than we expected?

We could even say that Blodeuedd never really betrayed anyone. She was simply being herself—her darker self, perhaps, but herself nevertheless. And the seeming betrayal can be laid at the door of those who failed to see her as a real person. To Lleu, Gwydion, and Math, she was but a wish-fulfillment, the illusion of their own projected animas.

By ignoring the import of Blodeuedd's questions as to how he might be killed, Lleu denied the reality that surrounded him. Why wasn't he thinking? Perhaps because he was listening to his primal brain rather than using his reason. His hand may have been skillful, but his mind was muddied by romantic love.

How, then, do we learn to deal with the woman within? How to bend the Lover's tumultuous, childlike dance into a symphony or a poem or an act of compassion? Gawain tried to fight his way through the Castle of Damsels, and the medieval poets seem uncertain as to whether he succeeded—or whether anyone can succeed through such tactics. Pwyll chased Rhiannon through the night without ever catching her, until he tried simple courtesy and asked her what she was about. This is a better solution—to approach one's inner woman with respect. Another Welsh hero, Manawyddan, accomplished the task by magic, and his was the more complete victory. In the *Mabinogion*,[14] Manawyddan is one of the children of Llyr. Clearly, he is the same figure as the ancient Irish sea god Manannan mac Lir, who gave the Isle of Man its name and whose apparition was still seen by Irish country folk as late as the eighteenth century. Though Rhiannon appears first as the Otherworldly bride of Pwyll, in this later story she becomes the wife of Manawyddan. But Manawyddan loses her, for Rhiannon, like the Greek Persephone, is abducted into the Underworld (i.e., the anima becomes buried in a man's unconscious). Manawyddan continues his life without his beloved Rhiannon, until one day as he works in his fields he notes that something has been eating his grain. He finally captures the culprit—a little field mouse. Then he does something very strange: he climbs to the top of a barrow mound, builds a small gallows for the mouse, and proceeds as if to hang the little creature for thievery. Three figures—priest, druid, and king—appear one by one, offering him ransom to save the tiny animal's life. But Manawyddan refuses all offers until the petitioner at last reveals himself as the Lord of the Underworld. The mouse is the Underworld Queen, as Manawyddan knows full well, and the only ransom he will accept for her is the return of Rhiannon (as well as her son Pryderi, another captive) from the nether regions.

Manawyddan certainly brought his anima up out of the unconscious, and we may take him as a prototype for the man who gains control over his inner feminine nature, so that he may manifest as an *effective* poet, musician, or caretaker rather than a captive of the women in his life—or a captive of his own unconscious. Manawyddan made the inner journey which, at the beginning of this chapter, we saw Perceval called upon to undertake. He descended to his own depths, and there he drank of the true cauldron of rebirth and inspiration which is the Grail, and which shows itself in this world as the Lover's chalice. But unlike Gawain, Manawyddan didn't pick up his sword and try to crash his way through the Castle of the Damsels. Sometimes the strategies of the Warrior simply do not work in the realm of the feminine! Instead, Manawyddan charmed her back with magic, and borrowed a page from the book of our next male archetype, the Magician or Druid.

Your inner Lover expresses itself positively if:

1. You are not afraid to be loving and affectionate in your relationships with others.

2. You naturally express yourself through the arts.

3. You are able to express your feelings clearly and without rage.

4. Women find your company pleasing and non-threatening.

5. Peace, harmony, and cooperation are essential to your way of life.

6. You can be compassionate, nurturing, and sympathetic even when your goals are challenged by others.

7. You see a therapist and are not afraid to hang out in the "self-help" section of your local bookstore.

8. Soft men like Alan Alda or Kevin Costner constitute role models for you.

9. To you, women are real people rather than objects.

10. You have a close relationship with spirit and nature.

Your inner Lover expresses itself negatively if:

1. You negate your own needs and desires for the sake of maintaining relationships with others.

2. You offer no resistance when others attempt to dominate you.

3. You idealize your lovers, and are often disappointed or deceived as a result.

4. Indulgence in drugs or alcohol constitute major escape mechanisms for you.

5. Your relationships are intense, dramatic, and short-lived.

6. The path of least resistance is the path you always travel.

7. You tend to be better at "leaving them" than "loving them."

8. Your relationships begin in a whirlwind of passion which flickers out all too soon.

9. You talk about your creativity constantly, but never do anything about it.

10. You are in love with love itself rather than with anyone in particular.

Notes

1. J. R. R. Tolkien, trans., *Sir Gawain and the Green Knight: Pearl and Sir Orfeo* (New York: Ballantine Books, 1980).

2. See Graves, *White Goddess*, 179–80, in which the principals in the Gawain story are linked with the archetypal combatants for the Goddess.

3. Gantz, trans., *Mabinogion*, 45–65.

4. New York: Macmillan Co., 1923 edition.

5. Squire, *Celtic Myth and Legend*, 140-2.

6. W.B. Yeats, "The Song of Wandering Aengus," in *The Collected Poems of W. B. Yeats* (New York: The Macmillan Company, 1970), 57–8.

7. Cross and Slover, *Ancient Irish Tales*, 370–421.

8. Denis de Rougemont, *Love in the Western World* (New York: Harper & Row, 1956).

9. The classic version is by Gottfried von Strassburg. (A recent edition is by A.T. Hatto, trans., *Tristan* [London, Penguin, 1967].) See also Joseph Bedier, *The Romance of Tristan and Iseult*, trans. Hilaire Belloc and completed by Paul Rosenfeld (New York, Vintage Books, 1945), and a Jungian interpretation in Robert Johnson, *We: Understanding the Psychology of Romantic Love* (San Francisco, Harper & Row, 1983).

10. Marie-Louise von Franz, *Puer Aeternus* (Santa Monica: Sigo Press, 1981).

11. Zimmer, *The King and the Corpse*, 186–8.

12. Gantz, trans., *Mabinogion*, 97–117.

13. Poem, untitled, by Marguerite Elsbeth.

14. Gantz, *Mabinogion*, 83–96.

CHAPTER 4

The Magician

In the last chapter, we left Lleu Llaw Gyffes, the archetypal lover, apparently killed by his enemy, Blodeuedd's Dark Lover. Goronwy had cast a magic spear at Lleu, wounding him in the back, and Lleu turned into an eagle and flew away. The magical preconditions for his death had been fulfilled. But was he really dead?

Gwydion of the Magic Harp didn't think so. He tracked a sow to an oak tree, under which the sow was seen to be feasting upon putrefying flesh. The flesh had dropped from a wounded eagle at the top of the tree.

So Gwydion sang three verses:

> *Between two lakes an oak tree grows,*
> *Dark the sky and dark the glen.*
> *If my words be true,*
> *This is from Lleu's feathers.*

An oak tree grows on a highland plain;
Nor rain nor heat can harm it.
Twenty branches, twenty skills,
And Lleu in the highest place.

On the slope an oak tree grows;
There the prince takes refuge.
If my words be true.
Lleu will fly down to my lap.[1]

With each verse the eagle comes a bit farther down the tree, and finally, as the song itself suggests, ends up in Gwydion's lap. Gwydion transforms the bird back into Lleu, heals him, and sends him forth again as a king.

This peculiar tale suggests a number of interpretations. Is Lleu, as some have believed, a sun god, and is Gwydion the primal force that charms summer out of winter? In any case, it is clear that the power of Gwydion's *words* brings Lleu back to life, or at least into full possession of himself and his consciousness.

We have already mentioned the connection between Gwydion, words, and trees. We may remember that it was Gwydion who fought the mythological Battle of the Trees in which the magic Ogham letters are mustered into service against an Underworld King. Gwydion and the forces of consciousness (words are conscious forces) triumph when Gwydion guesses the dark king's *name*.

The power of speech, of words, links the Warrior and the Magician, the sword and the wand. The Magician's power arises from the fact that he knows the sacred sound behind the workings of the universe, the vibration which brings all things into being. Thus Hermes, the master figure of Greco-Roman magic, is an incarnation of the Logos or Word. Thus the *rishis* of ancient India chanted great mantras in order to gain their power. Thus the Kabbalist learned the lore and legendry of the Hebrew alphabet, the primal matter from which Yahweh created the universe.

To know the secret *names* of things is to have power over them. And the Magician is the man of power.

Gwydion and Lleu

Power, however, is a tricky thing. One may have to suffer in order to attain it. Take, for example, the story of Odin, who bears a remarkable resemblance to our friend Gwydion of the Magic Harp. Just as Gwydion was the master of the sacred tree alphabet, the Ogham letters, so Odin was the master of the Runes, the old Norse alphabet of power. Odin had to lose an eye to gain the Runes. He also had to hang upside down for nine days and nights upon the World Tree, sacrificing "himself unto himself," until he could reach out screaming and grasp the Runes and all their knowledge. Do we have here an echo of Lleu's ordeal upon a similar tree?

The Magician or Druid is the wisdom-keeper of his people, and wisdom is not won easily. This archetype, like the King, denotes a mature man, one who has been to hell and back again. The "magic wand" or rod of power, the Grail Castle's lance, is the emblem of his successful struggle.

The lance corresponds to the suit of Wands in the Tarot. Wands signify movement and enterprise, new beginnings, energy, growth, and change. Though the lance itself may be yet another symbol of war, quarrel, and destruction, there is nevertheless an aura of renewal about the suit of Wands, for they are always in leaf, suggesting creativity, birth, and invention.

This emphasis upon creativity is fitting, for we may also regard the lance as a phallic symbol. In Tarot, Wands are linked with the element of fire, representing the spiritual plane and the creative forces of ardor, courage, spontaneity, and zeal. But in contrast to the heavenly (i.e. airy or cerebral) nature of the sword, the lance is an earthy implement, fashioned, like a wand or a staff, from the branch of a tree. By now we should be able to guess just which tree is intended here.

The Hindu *Upanishads* affirm that the branches of trees symbolize the five elements of ether, fire, water, air, and earth. Trees were also sacred to ancient European peoples. The Celts reverenced the oak and the hazel as trees of wisdom, and the Druids shaped a great deal of their philosophy around the sanctity of trees. Their magical alphabet was a tree alphabet, for each Ogham letter was associated with a particular tree, and gained its magical or divinatory meaning (at least in part) from its characteristic tree.[2] Thus the elm, hornbeam, willow, and birch joined the oak and the hazel as symbols of spiritual lore. The oak was especially sacred, for groves of oaks formed the ritual center of every community.

The significance of the tree cannot be separated from the notion of the "world axis." Most spiritual traditions of the ancient world recognize a World Tree which forms the symbolic center of the universe. The World Tree raises its vast branches well beyond the sphere of the Indo-European peoples with whom we are primarily concerned in this book. The tree in the Garden of Eden—prototype of the Kabbalistic mandala called the Tree of Life—is based upon an older World Tree which was prominent in the myths of Babylonian Semites. The Mayan pyramids were re-creations of a similar World Tree or World Mountain. To the pagan Norsemen the "tree at the center of the world" was a gigantic ash or yew named Yggdrasil, whose branches reached towards heaven and whose roots wound downward into hell. It was upon this tree that Odin crucified himself in order to gain the runic wisdom. And herein lies the richest clue to the meaning of the Magician's quest.

Among Siberian shamans, the journey to the Otherworld is imagined as an ascent up the trunk of the World Tree itself. The shaman, deep in his ecstatic trance, takes on the soul of his animal helper, typically a bird. In vision, he climbs the World Tree to the land of the gods. Here he will gain the wisdom, the knowledge which he must bring back to his people. It is this heavenly knowledge which will guide the tribe and determine its spiritual practice.[3] The Magician makes the same journey. He is master of the Otherworldly voyage. Like Gwydion, he can charm the solar wisdom, the eagle power, down from the heavenly land at the top of World Tree. He himself must undergo a painful initiation in order to gain this knowledge. One need only remember the severity of shamanic initiation among the tribes of the Great Plains to realize that no one becomes a Magician without some suffering. In Siberia, the shaman undergoing initiation often perceives himself as reduced to a skeleton. Gwydion seems to have undergone a similar process himself, for we may remember the old Welsh poem which speaks of him as being imprisoned in a "bone-fortress." In India, Tantric adepts meditate in graveyards and imagine themselves decaying in death, becoming skeletons. Herein we may see a nearly universal ritual of magical initiation.[4]

As a symbol of the axis of the world and hence the center of the life of the cosmos, the tree is emblematic of evolution and immortality. Like the Kabbalistic Tree of Life, it leads humankind to the Otherworld—though, like Yggdrasil, it has its ultimate roots in hell. And to hell we must go if we seek to master the magical path. Only when we have returned successfully may we take up the wand of power.

Now, perhaps, we may venture a guess as to why the lance in the Grail Castle drips with blood. This bleeding lance appears throughout medieval myth in various aspects. Galahad heals King Arthur by spreading blood from this same lance over his wound; Gawain sees the blood flowing from the lance caught by a silver vessel, the grail, as if for future use. When the Celtic tradition of the lance, originally the spear of the god Lugh, underwent a Christian transformation, the spear became associated with that of the Roman centurion Longinus that pierced the side of Jesus Christ during the Crucifixion. This intimates that the blood streaming from the tip of the lance has a sacrificial quality, that it is in fact "the blood of redemption." To redeem is to raise in stature, suggesting the idea of *rectitude*, the origin of which is associated with the word *royal* or *regal*, alluding to rulership and authority.

The Self is the one authority which rules—or is meant to rule—the personality with sovereign certainty. It grants kingship, leadership, control, and temporal power. It clearly defines mental activity and grants to intelligence a dominion over passion. This is the redeeming knowledge of the Self which the Magician has won on his bloody journey to the land of gods and demons. This is part of the knowledge that Perceval missed by his untoward silence in the hall of the Fisher King. By not asking questions, Perceval negated his own power and authority as well as displaying emotional immaturity and an umbilical attachment to his parents, especially his mother. By renouncing his own sacred individuality, he has opened himself to the pain of his inner wounds.

The Magician is a mature archetype. It is not a role that the young or the foolish may safely play. And in order to tap the vital power which animates both Magician and King, a man must touch the heart of another archetype, one we have not yet considered in this study—the Wild Man.

We have heard a great deal about the Wild Man of late in the context of the emerging men's movement.[5] A randy, phallic beast, he is both the source of and the principal actor in a man's drama of ecstasy, poetry, and illumination. Feral and overtly pagan, he is the fierce motive power behind every adolescent's haunting sense of personal magic. Later in this book, we shall meet this Wild Man in his characteristically Celtic guise as Cernunnos, the Lord of the Forest. But for now, let us merely note that the Wild Man lives close to Nature; in fact, we may even say that he is the man at one with all Nature.

Back in the Paleolithic era, shamans became one with Nature or the animal kingdom when they took up their animal masks, donning a pair of antlers to dance the hunting dance. As late as Elizabethan times, the May Day dances were led by a man clothed in green who wore antlers on his head. His ritual name was Robin Hood, which tells us that the forest outlaw of our childhood legendry is none other than the Wild Man of myth.

The Magician draws a great deal of his personal power from the primal power reservoir embodied in the Wild Man. In a little-known medieval work entitled the *Vita Merlini (Life of Merlin)*, the fabled magician of Arthurian lore is depicted as an unkempt recluse, a forest prophet who lives by a lonely spring. Before he retreats to the forest, Merlin instructs his wife Guendolena to forget about him and marry someone else. But when she actually does so, Merlin's reaction is both emotional and unexpected. He dons a headdress of antlers, magically calls the deer from the forest, and rides on the back of a stag into the wedding, disrupting it and scattering the guests. He flings his antlers at the groom, striking him dead. Merlin has become the Wild Man, the antlered god, a primal force which can charm the beasts from the wood or, as in this example, wreak chaos in the orderly activities of humankind.[6]

But a true Magician is not a man of wild disorder or chaos. It is, in fact, his task to master the holy chaos within him. It is to gain this mastery that he climbs to the Otherworld or hangs in pain upon the World Tree, a mere skeletal remnant of his old self. In most of the world's ancient spiritual traditions, the candidate for a magical vocation must undergo a rigorous program of training, whereby the energy of the Wild Man is brought under the individual's conscious control.

To train the Wild Man's energy into the appropriate channels of prophecy, divination, and magic was the special concern of the Druid priesthood among the ancient Celts. Unfortunately, we know far too little about the actual methods involved in Druidic training. The Roman conquerors made it their business to eradicate the Druids—though not necessarily for religious reasons, for the Romans were generally tolerant towards the faiths of the conquered. Caesar and his successors considered the Druids dangerous because they were *politically* powerful.

We do know that candidates for the Druidic priesthood were trained in natural, outdoor settings, in groves of oak trees, hidden valleys, or sometimes in caves. The course of training lasted for nineteen years, corresponding to a soli-lunar cycle called metonic. It was an oral training, in which the candidates were required to memorize long epic poems and complex lore.[7] There is some evidence that Druidic candidates were subjected to forms of sensory deprivation, locked in a cave or megalithic barrow so that only the internal workings of the memory would be stimulated.

But if many of the actual techniques of Druidic training have been lost to us, we may guess at their substance by considering similar disciplines. The philosophy of magic, as enunciated during Greco-Roman and Renaissance times, held that the mind brings all things into the formative universe. Words are conscious thoughts in action. All our actions have a resonance in the spiritual Otherworld. This is what the Magician knows. He knows that the mind must follow the heart, and that heart and mind are one. He understands the natural laws which define the true nature of energy, power, and matter, and why and how all of these are subordinate to our own ability to master the power of reason.

The kind of mental mastery sought by magicians moves the flow of conscious awareness from the Otherworld to our own physical world. It provides a correspondence or connecting link between the various planes of being which the Magician perceives. The Magician's knowledge of the correspondence or equivalence of any given thing in the universe enables him to know the unknowable, to see the unseen. Contemporary Hermetic philosophers, the heirs of the Renaissance magi as well as of the Druids and wise men who went before, perceive these correspondences or levels of being in terms of vibration.

Vibration, such as we produce when we utter a sound, is invisible energy. The lower the rate of vibration, the slower or more dense the object; the higher the vibration, the higher stands the object in the scale from gross matter to numinous spirit. The grossest forms of matter and the highest realms of spirit have in common the appearance of stillness. The Magician understands this and, consequently, trains his mind through meditative practice to be silent. Anyone who has attempted to meditate for the first time knows just how difficult it is to quiet the mental chatter which rises unbidden to the surface of the mind. Human consciousness is like a vast and roiling sea, and our jumbled thoughts may be compared to waves on the water. Practitioners of yoga assert that one must still the *citta* or "stuff" of the mind in order to attain the "seedless" state of *samadhi* or at-one-ment with the universe. This was the task of the old Celtic Druids as well.[8]

Ultimately, the Magician sees reality in terms of divine paradoxes which must be reconciled. In order to keep from losing his balance in extremes of "yes and no" or "right and wrong," he must learn to see things in shades of gray, in relative terms. All seeming pairs of opposites are to him but poles of one and the same thing. Evil may be transmuted into good when one realizes that neither one is a thing in itself; rather, they are opposite poles of the same thing. The Magician accomplishes his task by grasping the truth that there is motion in everything, including our mental states. By the use of the will— which the Magician believes to be divine in origin and which is symbolized by the lance or wand—he attains a degree of poise and mental stability which enables him to hold his central ground in the face of opposing belief systems. He knows that he must often move in contrary fashion to the ways of the world in order to keep from being tossed about in the ocean of collective fear patterns.

Every action brings about a reaction. Every cause has its effect. When we strive to practice the axiom of Rabelais which enjoins us to "Do what you will" with the intent of harming none, how can we be absolutely certain that our thoughts, words, and deeds are affecting no one but ourselves? For an active archetype like the Magician, it is always better to be the cause than the effect; but since nothing escapes universal law, he must be sure that his mind is in harmony with the Otherworld and the laws of Nature before he attempts to influence the lives of other creatures dwelling upon the earth (or on any other plane, for that matter).

A Magician knows that the physical, mental, and spiritual worlds work towards propagation, regeneration, and creation, and that every creature and thing has, inherent within its nature, both a subjective and an objective reality. A contemporary comic strip about a precocious magus-in-the-making and his stuffed tiger illustrates the duality which exists in all concepts. The tiger asks the boy if he has homework to do, and the boy responds that he thought the homework was "optional." When the tiger accuses the boy of being in denial, the child answers that he is simply selective about the realities he chooses to acknowledge. This is a humorous example of a very powerful concept: the idea that reality is a matter of perception. If we hone our perceptions to reflect the essential nature of any given thing, we become empowered by our knowledge of secrets which, thanks to our new standards of perception, now appear to be "hidden in plain sight."

The boy and the tiger remind us once again that the Magician or Druid, like Gwydion of the Magic Harp, is essentially a master of words and magic sounds. Gwydion, master of the Ogham alphabet, conquered the Underworld because he knew the secret names of things. Much of Druidic training was involved with learning such secret names.

But great power carries with it great responsibilities. And here we may find a clue to one of the weaknesses inherent in the Magician archetype. The Magician is always subject to a dark temptation—the temptation to use his power for selfish ends, to abuse his knowledge for the sake of personal self-aggrandizement. He has seen beyond the dualities of good and evil which move the rest of the world; he knows that these, too, are but words. The Magician sees everything in shades of gray. If he lacks integrity, those shades of gray may darken imperceptibly until they become black.

Pride and ego are perhaps the greatest culprits in the descent of a Magician into the darkness. Because he must take on powerful and visionary states of consciousness, the Magician must be trained to relinquish his ego at will, for it is perilous to carry his ego with him into the Otherworld. In Richard Wagner's operatic version of *Parsifal*, Klingsor is a knight who aspires to become one of the company of the Grail, the knights who guard the Fisher King. Rejected, he becomes angry and takes up the practice of black magic. In this version of the story, it is Klingsor rather than the sad Sir Balin who is responsible for the Grail King's wound. Klingsor fights the Grail King in battle, wounds him in the thigh, and steals the lance (i.e., the magic wand) out of the King's hands. It is Klingsor's damaged ego which makes of the Grail Kingdom a wasteland. His magic arts are subject to his pride and selfishness rather than being at the service of the people as a whole.

In Klingsor's story, we may see the mirror of ourselves. Science is the child of magic, and the only Magicians genuinely recognized by American society are the "wizards" of science, the researchers and inventors.[9] Lacking true spiritual concern and motivated only by a narrow, jingoistic patriotism or by their own desire for personal achievement, they are capable only of creating a technological wasteland. Like Klingsor, they hold the vital creative power of the society in their hands. But it is a power which they have stolen, rather than one freely given.

Klingsor, like all good sorcerers in all good fairy tales from Grimm to Tolkien, lives in a castle tower. The Magician who loses touch with the healing power of the unconscious is encased, like the Warrior, within a prison of his own making. The walls of his dark tower surround him as surely as the Warrior's suit of armor. Thus the Magician may become yet one more isolated man—cut off from his feelings, from intimacy, from life itself. The tower suggests a dark brooding isolation rather than the more physical isolation of the Warrior, for the Magician in a foul mood is nothing if not a brooder.

But upon what does he brood? The mind of a Klingsor may be filled with paranoia, with threats and dark spaces perceived on all sides of him—enemies to be conquered. The instinct for self-preservation is one of the strongest automatic responses shared by the collective mind. It has its source in our sense of personal identity, purpose, and motivation. When someone feels threatened, he usually does one of two things: he stands ready to fight or else runs away from the source of his trouble. This is the "fight or flight" syndrome (a buzz phrase in contemporary psychology) and is directly related to an excessive flow of adrenalin to the panic center in the brain.[10]

Stress—whether positive or negative, sudden or cumulative—is a precursor of anxiety. It is an affect, subjective and personal. The Magician is extremely prone to stress due to the very nature of his work: *he deliberately enters into a subjective realm wherein all his complexes and essential personal qualities must be revealed, laid bare, then consciously disintegrated only to be transmuted and reintegrated back into his personality.* If the Magician's "essential person" is filled with vulnerabilities, he may well begin to indulge in negative thinking habits, become high-strung or impulsive, feel emotionally drained, be at conflict with himself, or feel confused, frustrated, and bored. Anxiety may lead to fear, which, in turn, may lead to full-blown panic.

The word "panic" has its origins in the name of Pan, the goat-footed god of the ancient Greeks. Like the Celtic Cernunnos, Pan is a god of Nature and a primordial Wild Man. His name literally means "all." The wild places were Pan's home—the thickets and forests and mountains. He was forever falling in love with one woodland nymph after another, but he was always rejected because he was physically unattractive. Travelers hearing frightful sounds coming from the woods in the dead of night assumed that Pan was near. This primal terror of the dark and rural places led to the word "panic" as a definition of extreme fear.

In Native American and Siberian tribes the shaman was selected at an early age by virtue of his inability to become part of the herd mind—and we may suspect that the Druids looked for similar traits among their own young men. When a boy showed no interest in the hunt, sat brooding sullenly, lived in his daydreams, or displayed unwarranted fears, he was often recruited for training in the rites of passage particular to the attainment of shamanic knowledge.[11] Modern Western culture and society has lost touch with its pagan roots. We are trained from a very early age to fear the wild and barren places, the primal sources of the powers of Nature. Instead, we cling to noisy fast-food restaurants in brightly lit cities and never venture far from the TV screen and the pint container of Haagen Dazs.

In our own society, a world which denies the reality of magic and hence contains no accepted social role for Magicians (other than the scientists we mentioned above), it may be difficult to identify men who respond to this archetype. The Magician may be hidden in his wizard's tower almost anywhere—in any profession, in any walk of life. Sadly enough, almost the only way to recognize him is by way of his moods and psychological problems—the same anti-social sulk which marks the shamanistic candidate of traditional societies. It is no wonder that many men with a strong Magician archetype experience difficulties in making the transition from intellectuality to emotional beingness. Nevertheless, a fully functional Magician must be able to call upon both facets of his disposition in order to avoid a personality split.

As soon as an individual loses his sense of reality, he passes the thin boundary line which leads to "insanity." If he is neurotic, all is deemed right with the world and all is deemed wrong with the person himself; if he is psychotic, all is deemed right with the individual and it is the rest of the world which has gone mad. Either way, something has gone wrong between the inner or subjective self and the outer or objective personality. There is a tear in the individual's relationship with the world, a chaotic upset in his relationship with himself. A practicing Magician walks a very fine line between mystical illumination and schizoid, paranoid, or delusional behavior. When any of these pathologies occurs, the fragile ego separates or dissociates from the essence of the individuality, the Self. Disintegration of the personality has occurred, and the individual is at a loss as to how to put it all back together. This immersion in the dark Otherworld sea may have its roots in the body as well as the mind, for the food we eat, the air we breathe, and the lifestyles we live all have an effect on our biochemical make-up. The Magician needs to cultivate mental clarity founded on the wisdom of a heartfelt knowing.

Knowledge is power, control. If we are to be in control of our own lives, to be true Magicians, we must seek the required knowledge. When we experience pain, grief, and anxiety, we are presented with a challenge. When we are able to willingly accept the challenge, we may regain our poise, balance, and equilibrium on all levels—spiritual, mental, emotional, and physical.

But the darker reaches of egomania and schizophrenia are still not the only perils of the soul which the Magician must face. Both Wagner and his source, the medieval poet Wolfram von Eschenbach, depict Klingsor as the master of the Castle of Marvels which we have already briefly visited in the previous chapter. The Castle of Marvels is primarily a castle full of women, a Castle of Damsels, and hence a fitting metaphor for the unconscious world of a man.

As a medieval or modern descendant of Stone Age shamans, the Magician is a navigator upon the waters of the Otherworld, and the man who wields the magic wand may easily be swallowed up by the waves of the Otherworld sea, and drown therein—and a drowning man is dangerous to all those who may try to rescue him, for he has a tendency (whether conscious or otherwise) to take others down with him into the primordial depths.

Men tend to perceive the unconscious as feminine. The deeper layers of the unconscious, what Jung called the collective unconscious, are imaged as an ocean or sea. To sailors and landsmen alike, the ocean is "she," for we recognize in its vast depths the reflection of our own psychological depths. Similarly, it is most often a female figure who conducts a man to the Otherworld, as Beatrice guided Dante to Paradise, or as Celtic voyagers like Maelduin took ship over the sea to reach an Island of Women. The Lover, as we have seen, is all too likely to be seduced by the powerful anima, or "lady soul," which guides his life and makes him feel closer to women than to other men. If he drowns in the waters of his feminine side, he will spend his life as a *puer aeternus*, an "eternal boy" who can never quite detach himself from the feminine image. If he masters his inner feminine, he may become a great artist or performer, for all the creative arts emerge from the sea of the unconscious. This is why Joseph Campbell insisted[12] that the creative artists of this world were our contemporary shamans and makers of myth.

The Magician, like the Lover, must maintain a similarly close connection with the "lady soul" within, for magic, like creativity, comes forth from the unconscious, and there is little difference between poet and mystic. If the Magician must be a Warrior when he wields the wand and sword of the Creative Word, he must be a Lover when he voyages over the seas of intuition or psychic phenomena.

In the last chapter, we considered the case of Manawyddan, a successful blend of Lover and Magician. Less successful in blending the wand and the chalice was Merlin, the most famous magician of all. Despite his magical prowess and mastery of the words of power, he himself fell victim to the lure of the unconscious and was swallowed up by it. The story of his fall exists in numerous versions, but the outlines are always the same. Merlin encounters a young woman, and falls madly in love with her. There is something Otherworldly about her; sometimes she is said to be a magical creature herself, connected to the isle of Avalon. At any rate, she longs to learn the secrets of Merlin's magical powers, and, because he is in love, he sets out to teach her. Once she has learned everything she needs to know, she betrays him. She locks him away forever, sometimes in a rock, sometimes in an oak tree (fitting fate for a Druid). In one version, Merlin falls asleep beneath a whitethorn tree, and the girl—called Niniane in this story—weaves a spell around him. When he wakes up, he appears to be in a magical tower rather than beneath a tree. Where, in fact, is he? In the Castle of Damsels once again![13] In many fairy tales, it is the young woman who is held captive in a tower by an evil magician. Here we have a curious reversal—the Druid held captive in a tower by the girl.

Women have often banded together to present a united front. In Neolithic times, women were revered for embodying the life-force of the Great Goddess. Today, women are once again discovering the roots of their ancient spirituality and participating in their own rituals. This is sometimes quite threatening to the contemporary man

who, for five thousand years, has enjoyed a starring role in a predominantly patriarchal society. The Warrior and the King either
remain oblivious or indulge in mockery over this turn of events, for
they believe the star role is simply their due. The Lover, like men in
Neolithic times, genuinely reveres women and is supportive of their
goals. But the Magician is filled with ambivalence about the female
power. He is not polarized towards one end of the spectrum or the
other—he knows better. And there are frightening images buried
deep in those overactive primordial memory banks of his.

What the Magician remembers is something which contemporary advocates of Goddess spirituality would prefer to forget—or
even deny. Theorists like Riane Eisler or Marija Gimbutas[14] insist
that there is no evidence of human sacrifice in Neolithic times,
though this is not precisely true. Beneath many stone circles of the
British Isles—Late Neolithic or Early Bronze Age sites eagerly
claimed by Goddess worshippers as their own—lie buried the
remains of apparent sacrificial victims of both sexes, children as
well as adults.[15]

Contemporary Goddess worshippers also cite Robert Graves'
book *The White Goddess* as one of the most influential books in their
movement, and this important work (like its predecessor, Frazer's
Golden Bough) is based on the fundamental premise that men were
ritually (and regularly) sacrificed by women in Neolithic times.
The Goddess culture was both revered and feared by men living in
those times, and it is this primal fear which sleeps in men's souls, a
fear akin to the primal terror awakened in women by recollection
of the late medieval witch hunts or Burning Times. To the Magician, the primordial images are not all that far from the surface.

As we will investigate more fully in the next chapter, the idea
of the Sacrificial King is a common theme in the spirituality of
ancient Europe. The sacrifice is made to the Great Goddess in her
aspect as Harvest Mother, in order to ensure a fruitful harvest, for
it is she who makes the crops grow tall. If the Harvest Mother is not
properly reverenced throughout the growing season, then the
crops may wither and die. As late as the last century, some villages
maintained an old custom wherein, after the harvest, the man to
give the last stroke at threshing was named Son of the Corn

Mother. He was tied up in the last sheaf of corn, the symbolic Corn Mother which has been shaped into the form of a woman. In mock ceremony the man was beaten, jeered at, carried through the village, and thrown upon the local dung heap. In other parts of Europe a stranger entering the village around harvest time might be greeted by a crowd of reapers who formed a circle around him and sharpened their sickles, while the leader recited:

> The men are ready,
> The scythes are bent,
> The corn is great and small,
> The gentleman must be mowed.[16]

A very nice reception for the casual tourist, whose primordial brain may well "remember" that what is about to be "mowed" is his head or testicles! In the popular novel *Harvest Home*,[17] Thomas Tryon approaches the practice of male sacrifice in grand archetypal fashion. The story takes place in a small town in Connecticut, to which a family from New York has relocated in search of a safe, idyllic rural lifestyle. The man of the family is enthralled at first with the colorful local customs and folklore. But in the end he discovers that this seemingly innocuous society of matriarchal pagans practices midnight rituals in the cornfields which include castrating the youthful harvest lord with a sickle and tearing him to pieces—a ritual in which the protagonist's own wife gladly learns to participate.

One writer on the men's movement[18] has described how his men's group was invited to a ceremony by a group of pagan feminists. Upon arriving, the men were surprised to find that the object of the ritual was a large wicker man with penis erect. The women set the penis on fire and danced around the burning man, screaming insults at his flaming member. At several recent astrology conferences in Santa Fe, New Mexico, feminist astrologers have introduced the theme of the castration of Ouranos (the planet Uranus). Ouranos was the original sky-god of Greek myth. He became a tyrant, so the earth-mother Gaia persuaded his son Cronos to lie in wait and cut the sky-father's balls off. The men in the audience (all of them "soft" New Age men, inasmuch as none of the local rednecks would be caught dead at an astrology conference) were visibly disturbed the first time the theme arose. "What exactly does this mean?" they asked the speaker, as if suspecting that they might be next on the list to sacrifice their testicles without knowing why.

But there really is no reason why. As the original creative force, Ouranos may be symbolized by the Magician's wand which brings all things into manifestation. When he was castrated, his life-force was shattered, his self-assertion and self-preservation instincts destroyed. Cronos took away his *virility*—at the behest of the Goddess. It is this sense of power and virility which is symbolized by Cernunnos, the horned magister of pagan rites who dances at the center of the Otherworld and who is the original Wild Man lurking beneath the Magician's power. It is a power which every man possesses by right, but which every man sacrifices when he loses his sense of identity in the feminine unconscious.

Is it any wonder that, following the Goddess era of Neolithic times with its rites of male sacrifice, the men eventually decided to strike back and reclaim their own power? The collective unconscious works according to its own time frame, and five thousand years may be just a drop in the bucket—five thousand years between the time when the first patriarchal Indo-European tribes poured out of southern Russia to overcome the Goddess societies of southeastern Europe (c. 3,500 BC) and the time when patriarchal culture reached a grim culmination in the late Middle Ages. During the 1300s, the continent of Europe entered what has been called the Burning Times, when many innocent women of all ages were tortured and burned for witchcraft and heresy, whether real or fabricated. The pendulum had shifted from Goddess worship and male sacrifice to complete male supremacy and the destruction of the feminine principle. A primordial terror of the darkness (which is nothing more than our ignorance of any given person, place, or thing) loomed in the minds of men, with women and their knowledge of ancient healing crafts as the source of the panic. While witches danced with Cernunnos deep in the heart of the local forest, Catholic priests and inquisitors danced around the burning flames as bewildered wives and mothers screamed in agony. The dark Magician was born once again, and humankind has fostered his reign of terror throughout the ensuing five centuries. Though the vehicle has changed, the trip is unfortunately the same—men and women continuing to interact in dichotomous, oppositional ways.

Carl Jung commented upon the swing of the historical pendulum in relationship to the eternal "battle of the sexes." He predicted that feminism and the emerging women's rights movement would, in its early years, swing towards one extreme of the pendulum's field of motion, thus producing an adverse, even hateful reaction against men. He also surmised that the pendulum would, in time, rest in the middle. In the present day, the pendulum often swings so fast that it appears to be standing still! Perhaps someday the Magicians of this world and their female counterparts can raise their vibrations so high that the pendulum will truly rest at the still point in the middle.

Because of his special awareness, the Magician must always be wary of the attractive power of the unconscious, of psychic phenomena, of love and sex. These feminine aspects of Nature have the power to swallow him up, to rob him of the sharp masculine skills of discrimination (the Warrior's sword) which are absolutely necessary for the working of his magic. And herein lies another clue to the particular brand of male isolation experienced by the Magician—he is frequently much better off staying clear of relationships altogether. His connectedness with the Otherworld constitutes the primary feminine component of his soul. If he goes any deeper into the ocean of feminine consciousness, he may well drown like the Lover. The Lover, of course, is the only male archetype which *isn't* isolated—the Magician shares his aloneness with the Warrior and the King. He has to watch his step around women.

Though Merlin himself fell victim to the dark waters of the unconscious, he is not remembered *primarily* for his entrapment by the feminine—rather, he is most familiar to us as the teacher of King Arthur. And here we may find a clue as to why the Druid or Magician must wield, at one and the same time, the Warrior's sword of words, the Lover's cup of female power, and his own magic wand. Because only by embodying all these things may he fulfill his destiny as teacher of the Sacred King.

Your inner Magician expresses itself positively if:

1. You are inclined to take it easy and go with the flow.
2. You treat others as you yourself would wish to be treated.
3. You believe that the experience of life is a gift to be shared.
4. You attempt to contribute to the task of making the world a better place.
5. You question authority and trust your intuition.
6. You practice reverence for all life.
7. A higher spiritual power or energy (however you may wish to define it) is the guiding force of your existence.
8. You live by your own unique standard of values.
9. Achieving spiritual grace and developing a compassion for human frailty are among your primary goals.
10. You make a conscious effort to develop wisdom and understanding.

Your inner Magician expresses itself negatively if:

1. Your only concern is for yourself.
2. Your desire for personal power sometimes overwhelms your willingness to live in harmony with Nature.
3. You want it all, any way you can get it.
4. You regard it as your duty to obey the "laws of the land" even when they go against the grain of cosmic justice.
5. Fear of death is your primary motivation.
6. You feel a need to achieve mastery over persons, places or things.

7. Nurturing your ego or personality is more important than living by your principles.

8. You regard yourself as the arbiter of wisdom in any group in which you may find yourself.

9. Your desire for deep knowledge is actually based upon your need to control.

10. You manipulate people by withholding information which might help them achieve their own empowerment.

Notes

1. *Mabinogion,* paraphrase by Kenneth Johnson of several translations.

2. Edred Thorsson, *The Book of Ogham* (St. Paul, MN: Llewellyn Publications, 1992).

3. Mircea Eliade, *Shamanism: Archaic Techniques of Ecstasy* (Princeton: Princeton-Bollingen, 1972).

4. Ibid., 33–66.

5. Especially in Bly, *Iron John.*

6. Nikolai Tolstoy, *The Quest for Merlin* (Boston: Little, Brown & Co., 1986), 74–5.

7. Stuart Piggott, *The Druids* (New York: Thames & Hudson, 1975), 104–8.

8. Tadhg MacCrossan, *The Sacred Cauldron: Secrets of the Druids* (St. Paul, MN: Llewellyn Publications), 1991.

9. Moore and Gillette, *King, Warrior, Magician, Lover,* 97–118.

10. Billie Jay Sahley, *The Anxiety Epidemic* (San Antonio, TX: Watercress Press, 1986).

11. Eliade, *Shamanism,* 3–66.

12. Joseph Campbell, with Bill Moyers, *The Power of Myth* (New York: Doubleday, 1988), 99.

13. Zimmer, *The King and the Corpse,* 194–6.

14. Riane Eisler, *The Chalice and the Blade* (San Francisco: Harper and Row, 1988), and Marija Gimbutas, cited in Eisler, passim.

15. Aubrey Burl, *Stone Circles of the British Isles* (New Haven, CT: Yale University Press, 1976), 183–4, 234, 271–2.

16. Frazer, *The Golden Bough*, 425–31.

17. New York: Alfred A. Knopf, 1977.

18. Aaron R. Kipnis, *Knights Without Armor* (Los Angeles: Jeremy P. Tarcher, 1991), 62–4.

CHAPTER 5

The King

In a society where "patriarchy" has become a term of censure and insult, the King shares with the Warrior an uncomfortable position. In fact, the word "king" may often be regarded as a mere synonym for "tyrant" or even "male oppressor." The Lover and the Magician are occasionally excused from these labels by virtue of their innate sensitivity, their closeness to their feminine side. But the King stands (with the Warrior beside him) as a glowering symbol of male authoritarianism.

If the Magician is a difficult man to place in modern society, the King is easy. We all know who he is. President of the corporation, sports hero grown a bit paunchy, or mayor of the town, his is the house on the hill, the figurative castle from which he surveys his domain. The biggest New Year's parties are held at his house, and he is noticed when he strides out upon the local golf course. He has money. He has mastered the material world, at least within the confines of his own business or community.

Must we therefore assume that he is also a male chauvinist pig, a closet alcoholic, and cruel to both his children and his employees? He may or may not be any of these things. But whether he is a pillar of virtue or a shadowy tyrant, the King, too, has his pain, his wound. He is not by any means a simple, one-dimensional being. In fact, on one level the King is symbolic of the Self, the inner core of a man's being, and some male mythologists[1] feel that the other archetypes— Warrior, Lover, and Magician—evolve *out of* the King. For the King is nothing less than the sun, and the sun is a universal symbol for what yogis call the *atman*, the transcendent Self that lies within.

The sun has been worshiped and deified throughout history, at least in the mythological era. Sun gods are typically endowed with the gift of knowledge that results from spiritual vision. Helios-Apollo was known as the eye of Zeus in Greece; Surya, the sun god of India, was the eye of Varuna; in Persia the sun was the eye of Ahura Mazda and in Egypt the all-seeing eye of Ra. In Indo-European myth, the king of the gods possesses the same all-encompassing vision as does the sun. He sits upon his throne on the highest of mountains and surveys the world. Thus Zeus gazed upon the world from the top of Mount Olympus, and Odin surveyed Middle Earth from his throne on a peak in Asgard. It is probable that the Celts also recognized such a sky king, though time and circumstance have robbed us of the original myth. Math the Ancient, the Magician King of the *Mabinogion*, may have been such a god, and the throne from which he dispensed erratic justice and occasional wisdom was perhaps a seat of vision like that occupied by Zeus or Odin.

In ancient times, earthly kings were regarded as incarnations of the sun, like the pharaohs of Egypt—and in fact Louis XIV was still thinking mythologically as late as the seventeenth century when he called himself the Sun King. By virtue of its central position in our solar system, the sun in astrology signifies the ego, creativity, pride, purpose, good judgment, will power, and vitality, all qualities associated with the archetype of the King as well as his compatriot the Warrior. We should remember that the Warrior's weapon is the sword, a weapon associated with air or heaven. A Lover may grow into a Magician; a Warrior grows into a King.

The Warrior, as we have seen, has strong symbolic associations with the element of air and with the power of thought or speech which that element symbolizes. The King, too, is a master of this element, as is clear from the fact that so many kings of the gods are also lords of the sky.

Consider Zeus, the Roman Jupiter, for instance. In Greek myth, this king of the gods also rules over all things associated with the turmoil of the heavens: dark clouds, thunder, and bolts of lightning are his domain. And if medieval and Renaissance astrologers linked their earthly kings with the sun, they also gave consideration to Jupiter as a most kingly planet indeed. Jupiter was the planet they most often studied when attempting to predict the destiny of kings and the affairs of state.

Jupiter was sometimes known as Jove, and our word "jovial" is derived therefrom. A true King should be a man of "jovial" disposition—generous, expansive, and optimistic. Pryderi, the son of Pwyll and one of several Magician Kings in the *Mabinogion*, displayed such qualities. When Manawyddan son of Llyr found himself bereft and homeless following the death of his brother King Bran, Pryderi demonstrated his open-hearted goodness by offering him the authority and enjoyment of the seven domains he had himself inherited from his father. He even bestowed upon Manawyddan the hand of his mother Rhiannon in marriage.[2] King Arthur was philosophical and truth-seeking as well as enthusiastic—the order he founded, the Knights of the Round Table, was dedicated to the highest ideals of chivalry.

If the King Jupiter of astrological lore is optimistic and magnanimous, he is also self-sacrificing, noble, compassionate and sympathetic. Pwyll of Dyved (some of whose story has been told in the two previous chapters) endured much, both *for* and *from* his people, when he descended into the Underworld to battle the fearsome Havgan, bringing light to the populace and releasing them from the fear of death. Again, he volunteered to sit on the great barrow mound of Gorsedd Arberth, either to receive blows or to see a wonder (whichever happened first): thus he taught his people to know courage and the realization of dreams.[3]

But a Jupiterian king may also be judgmental, tactless, and dishonest. Conor mac Nessa, King of Ulster and patron of the great Warrior Cuchulain, came to grief with his company of heroes over a woman. Her name was Deirdre, and she was so beautiful that Conor kept her hidden in the woods, concealed from all other eyes. But the three sons of Usnach discovered her whereabouts, and she fell in love with one of them, named Naoise. Naoise and Deirdre fled with the sons of Usnach, and Conor's jealousy sat festering. At last he invited them back to Ireland, ostensibly to forgive. But his real plan was to trap them in the great house dedicated to the Red Branch, Conor's brotherhood of heroes. There he attacked them. Because Conor had given his kingly word to protect the exiles, many of his Red Branch warriors believed he had done wrong to play such a fatal trick on them. Some of the Red Branch joined the attack on the sons of Usnach, but others refused. And though Conor got his way by making an end of the sons of Usnach (and, sadly enough, of Deirdre as well), his brotherhood of champions had broken apart and nothing could bring it back together again. The Warriors of the Red Branch had lost faith in Conor's integrity as a Sacred King.[4]

The dark King, victim of jovial Jupiter's selfish shadow, is secretive, victimizing, and short-sighted. Mallolwch, King of Ireland, set forth in grandeur and in glory to ask that Branwen, daughter of Llyr, become his wife. But Branwen's quarrelsome brother Evnissyen was greatly displeased that he had not been present for the betrothal ceremonies. He took his revenge by mutilating the beautiful horses given to the sons of Llyr by the Irish king (a mythic theme which has been given an eerie modern treatment in Peter Shaffer's play *Equus*). Mallolwch showed his dark side by punishing Branwen for the deed, treating her poorly as a wife rather than confronting Evnissyen in manly fashion. In time, Branwen became so abused that her brothers, Bran and Manawyddan (as well as the evil but ultimately heroic Evnissyen) were forced to come to her rescue.[5]

The King may be like the sun or like Jupiter. He may be substance or shadow. But all ancient sources agree that his proper symbolic metal is gold, the sun-colored metal which is still so highly prized by the rich, the famous, and those who simply aspire to be chic. Throughout the esoteric tradition of the Western world (as well in India), gold is the metal which is symbolically associated with the sun by magicians and astrologers, and the sun is the spiritual life center of both the human and the celestial universe, the central luminary of our solar system. Human consciousness is itself a microcosmic manifestation of the sun's vital power. Sun gods (and goddesses) are among the most universal of deities. The Welsh Lleu Llaw Gyffes and his Irish counterpart Lugh may well have been sun gods, and Grania, whose love for Dermot O'Dyna brought sorrow to the court of Finn MacCool, seems to have originally been a solar goddess of sorts.

Hermetic alchemical treatises as well as the Ayurvedic medical texts of India regard gold as the kingly metal and ascribe to it many healing properties. And whether through actual physical proximity or simply through the power of symbolic evocation, gold ore does in fact seem to heighten our awareness. Praised by the alchemists as a malleable, "projective," and transformative agent, gold is said to excite the dynamic or masculine aspect of human nature by directing the universal life power into the field of human sensory experience. Gold has been universally regarded as the essence of the solar power in physical form, initiating and transmitting energy in the semblance of will and desire from the gods to earthly monarchs, and thence through the King to the people and the land for which he is the visible symbol.

The King, then, is in one very important sense a symbol of the ultimate and absolute source of a man's being. His throne lies at the center of all things. The Magician may climb the World Tree in search of wisdom, as we noted in the last chapter, but the King is the World Tree itself. Babylonian ziggurats as well as Mayan pyramids were built as images of the great World Mountain or Tree, the center of the universe. These sacred sites were the stages upon which ancient kings performed their rituals—rituals which were intended to renew the kingdom as a whole.[6] The Celts held a similar belief, for old descriptions of the High King's court on the hill of Tara make it clear that Tara was more than just a fortress—it was a cosmogram, a carefully constructed geomantic image of the universe itself.[7]

As we can see, the King has his depths. In order to explore those depths, let us return to Perceval's initial experience in the Grail Castle.

The archetype of the King is symbolized by the silver serving dish. Scholars who equate the Four Grail Treasures with the Four Treasures of the Tuatha de Danaan link the dish with the Stone of Fal. This great stone was brought to Ireland by the gods themselves, and its magic was this: the stone cried out whenever a true King stood upon it. No man could become High King of Ireland until he had placed his foot upon the Stone of Fal and the Druids had clearly heard the stone cry out. This was part of the coronation ritual of ancient Ireland—a ritual which is still evident in Britain up to the present day, for the old Scottish "Stone of Scone" is still part of the coronation chair in Westminster Abbey. Thus we may say with certainty that if the Grail Castle's serving dish is the spiritual descendant of the Stone of Fal, then surely it is the emblem of the inner King. But what does the dish really signify?

Once again we may turn to the Tarot, where the symbol of the dish is mirrored in the suit of Pentacles or Coins, the Diamonds of the standard card deck. The pentacle is circular in form and engraved with a pentagram or five-pointed star, symbol of magic, the five senses and extremities of man, as well as the five elements of nature (ether, fire, water, air, and earth). The pentagram is also an instrument of protection. In medieval times pentacles or talismans were typically inscribed with magical formulae. It is clear that the pentacle, like the Grail Castle itself, is a kind of mandala or cosmogram. In the center of the squared circle of the Grail Castle we find yet another symbolic circle, the deepest layer of the Self we have thus far reached. This is the King.

In Renaissance and Reformation times, the pentacles of the Tarot were imagined as coins of gold, while the dish in the Grail Castle is silver. Similarly, we have seen that the grail itself, as a symbol of the Goddess and the moon, ought to be silver, whereas the Grail Legend tells us it is gold. Unlike silver, gold does not tarnish, and perhaps there is a clue here as to why the grail must be fashioned of gold. Liquid substances, whether blood or water, will erode matter over time. But the life-force of a King must not

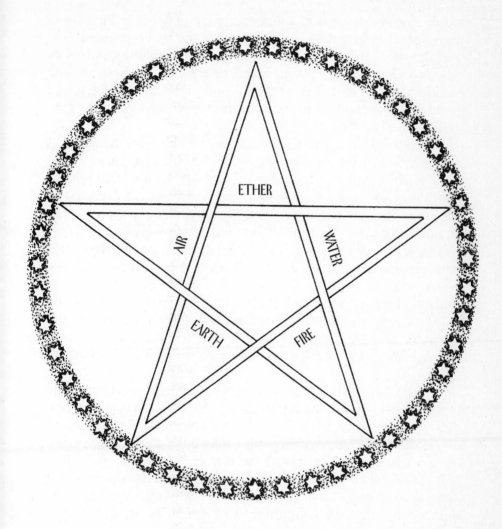

Pentagram with Five Elements

erode. It must endure over time. Is it the life-force itself which the grail contains?

In any case, there is an interpenetration of silver and gold, sun and moon implied here, which suggests the union of masculine and feminine elements, and we shall explore this union farther when we deal with the mystic marriage between the King and the Goddess of the Land. But for now, we may surmise that the magic circle of the pentacle is to some degree representative of the sun, and hence of the "sun-king."

Despite all these solar associations, the Pentacles of the Tarot are regarded as pre-eminently a symbol of the element of earth. Earth is *physical* matter, comprised of that which is real and solid to man's limited sensory perception. Practicality and dependability are associated with this elemental quality, along with a certain amount of caution, conservatism, and possessiveness. In other words, when we are connected with the earth element we expect what we see, hear, touch, taste, and smell to be tangible realities. We expect the earth to remain solid and still beneath our feet (unless we happen to live in California). However, change is the only constant, and the only true foundation of being is essentially spiritual. So an overly strong identification with the physical plane may leave us blind, deaf, insensitive, and dumb in the face of the Otherworld.

A man with a strong inner King typically relates very strongly to what we might call the "earth plane"—he excels at business, politics, and the accumulation of material substance. The notion of descending into his psychic depths may be frightening to such a man, for he is literally "out of his element"—i.e., his element is earth, not water. But make the descent he must, for he must become a Lover—a Lover whose mystic bride is the land itself, or, in modern terms, the community and society in which the King lives, breathes, and has his being.

An old Irish story[8] tells how Niall of the Nine Hostages (reigned 379–405 AD), ancestor of the O'Neills, became High King of Ireland. Because the old king had five sons, the young princes were forced to undergo a number of tests to determine which one should reign. They were all sent out hunting. They killed a boar and lit a fire.

Then they were seized with a great thirst and went in search of water. Each one in turn came upon an old woman seated next to a well. The woman was hideous, with leprous skin, hair like a horse's mane, long green fingernails and mossy green teeth like the huge fangs of an animal. The water in the well was fresh and cool, but the old woman would not allow the king's sons to drink from it unless they kissed her first. Four of the brothers fled in terror. Only Niall agreed to kiss the hideous hag. Not only that, he agreed to lie with her as well. And when he did so, the hag was transformed into the most beautiful woman anyone had ever seen. And she told Niall, "Lordship is mine, for I am Sovereignty." She named him High King and gave him to drink of the waters of the magic well.

This story contains the memory of what must once have been an ancient pagan ritual: the marriage of the High King to the Goddess of Sovereignty, Goddess of the Land. When a new High King was elected in ancient Ireland, his accession to the throne was celebrated with a great feast, the "Feast of Tara" or, in Gaelic, *Feis Temhra*. Interestingly enough, the word *feis* or "feast" also signifies sexual union.[9] The High King probably celebrated his ritual marriage to the Goddess of the Land or Sovereignty during this festival, perhaps through sexual congress with a high priestess. This ritual marriage is found in myths the world over. It is called the *hieros gamos* or "mystic marriage" and appears in Gnostic theology, Hindu Tantra, and Western alchemy, among other traditions. In a personal or psychological sense it often signifies the union of male and female elements within the individual psyche. But behind its individual meaning lies a more universal one: the union of the King, the male principle or Logos, with the Goddess or female principle as personified in the land.

Because the health of the land is dependent upon the vitality of the King, he lives not for himself, but for others. He is married to the land.

But the problem is, a King must be perfect.

The old Irish epic of *The Second Battle of Moytura* tells how the gods, the Tuatha de Danaan, came to Ireland.[10] Their king was the god Nuada, who led the Tuatha to victory over the aboriginal Fomorians. But he lost an arm in the battle, and, because of this, he was forced to relinquish the kingship to a Fomorian named Bres. In ancient Ireland, no man who possessed any physical blemish, however small, could become the king.

This overwhelming insistence upon perfection reveals to us, in a psychological sense, the modern King's secret sorrow: he is addicted to perfection. He has to have the prettiest wife, the smartest children, the best cars and motorboats, the finest array of home improvements. He must be strong, able to work eighty hours a week while lesser men conk out at forty.

When the King is less than perfect—as every human being is less than perfect—his faults have repercussions above and beyond his own personal pain. As we have noted, the kings of the ancient world were responsible for the health of the entire kingdom. Every year, the Babylonians enacted a New Year's Festival which replayed the original cosmic drama. Once again the great god Marduk defeated the forces of chaos and put the universe in order. The King acted the chief part in this festival, for he was himself the emissary of Marduk to the lower world, the intermediary of the gods upon earth. The Egyptians, like other African peoples, placed the pharaoh himself at the center of annual rites of renewal wherein he was forced to prove that he was still vital and potent, thus still entitled to rule as the divine intermediary.[11]

And what happens when the King, less than perfect, fails to renew his kingdom? The whole land suffers. Bres, who gained the throne of Ireland because of Nuada's wound, was a stingy and ungenerous King. During his reign Ireland fell under a kind of blight. The cows would not give milk; the weather remained dark and dismal.

The Grail King lies wounded, suffering in his castle. This is why the whole Grail Kingdom is a wasteland.

Any place may fall barren and become a wasteland when the quality of enlightened leadership is absent. In Larry McMurtry's novel *The Last Picture Show*,[12] a small town in Texas slowly dies, its spirit and its integrity decaying over time after the death of its one outstanding man. No wonder Robert Bly claims that the spiritual poverty of modern society is not due to the presence of patriarchs so much as it is due to the absence of *enlightened* patriarchs![13]

The King is a figurehead who represents his people; ideally he may serve as their role model. If the King is sick, then the whole consciousness of a society, a nation, a culture will suffer. Just as the earth absorbs the light of the sun and is nurtured by it, the kingly essence which symbolizes the highest potential of man is absorbed by and nourishes a people. The sick King cannot nourish the people, for the land around him lies waste, like the land of the Fisher King:

> *Here is no water but only rock*
> *Rock and no water and the sandy road...*
> *Here one can neither stand nor lie nor sit*
> *There is not even silence in the mountains*
> *But dry sterile thunder without rain*
> *There is not even solitude in the mountains*
> *But red sullen faces sneer and snarl*
> *From doors of mudcracked houses*[14]

Because the King represents the royalty and grandeur of the solar world, he must be able to integrate both the heart and the mind, the silver and the gold, by displaying mindful compassion toward the people and the land.

Sometimes it would seem that we as a society are collectively foolish to follow the dictates of another all-too-human being just because he happens to be sitting on the King's archetypal throne. There are many sick Kings (and Queens!) governing the nations of the world today who have not succeeded in marrying the silver to the gold. They are mere mortals who, in their ignorance, believe that they are here on the planet in their elevated positions of royal sovereignty to assist Nature in her wildish plan. They think that the world may somehow fail without their help. We need but gaze around at the kingdoms laid waste in order to see what the sick King's high-tech meddling has wrought. Unable to imagine life as a good time without cars and refrigerators, he ignores the hole in the ozone layer. The rain forests—our main source of oxygen for the planet as well as home to thousands of unknown medicinal plants, rare and exotic animals, and aboriginal tribes—are quickly being burned or cut down, or else they are dying from unusual atmospheric causes. Nuclear waste is buried beneath the earth with no thought for future generations, and weapons are created for war while people are hungry, sick, and homeless.

The sick Kings who govern our planet spend their waking hours thinking of new and improved ways to annihilate the people, creatures, and things indigenous to the land. In the United States, the Bush administration spent four years engaged in military build-up and eliminating broccoli from the White House. The most popular philosophy of life was: "He who dies with the most toys wins." Vice President Quayle (an aspiring sick King) fought the head of the Environmental Protection Agency regarding the preservation of wildlife and the primacy of corporate enterprise. Perhaps Mr. Quayle has another planet to go to! Just before leaving office, President Bush decided in favor of the EPA, suggesting that even sick Kings may be healed.

Increasing public and planetary awareness insists that we learn to recognize the wreck and refuse of the sick King for what it is— greed, separatism, self-aggrandizement, and other unsavory by-products of the imbalance between emotional and intellectual development. The King's ability to reason objectively on behalf of his people is a great boon to humankind when it is inspired by feeling, when it is used to purify and refine. It is part of the King's sacred trust to sift through the dross of the old order, preserve what is valuable and beneficial, then jettison the rest. To survive and endure the illness which, thanks to a surfeit of sick Kings, has transformed our own Grail Kingdom into a wasteland, we must learn to invoke the healthy sacred King within ourselves. We must *become* Kings, willing to take up the burden of ruling the land and all its inhabitants with our hearts as well as our minds. We must learn to base our decisions upon some higher principle than that represented by basic instinct alone. In order to accomplish this, the King within us must learn to use the wand of intuition and the grail cup of feelings with as much skill as he wields the sword of the mind and the golden pentacle of worldly wealth.

But, as we have noted, the King is out of his element when immersed in the watery realm of his feelings. Sea kings are often sick Kings. Greek Poseidon was a slave to his stormy rages, and

Bran, son of the sea god Llyr, suffered decapitation—though his mind survived as an oracle. Another son of Llyr, Manawyddan (the Welsh incarnation of the Irish sea god Manannan), spent the night on a barrow mound and woke to find his kingdom a wasteland.

Sea kings personify the oceanic depths within us, the uncharted waters of the unconscious mind in its regressive or chaotic state. Lakes and fresh rain may be considered fertile sources of potential growth, but the sea represents something unknown—something which may either nurture us or manifest as a destructive blight.

Lleu Llaw Gyffes, the wounded King who, in the form of an eagle, was coaxed down from the World Tree by the Magician Gwydion, was said to have been born of the moon goddess Arianrhod by a mysterious sea god—his shadowy brother Dylan dove back into the sea at birth. Thus Lleu may be considered yet another sea king. Certainly he suffered accordingly. Cursed by his own mother, tricked by his flower maiden, injured almost unto death by Goronwy's spear, Lleu flew away and isolated himself amidst the stench of his own rotting flesh. Only when Gwydion reminded him of his own worthiness and the beauty that still lingered in his heart did Lleu trust that his self-imposed exile of mortal (or perhaps we should say moral) decay could end, that he could be healed and set to rights. And so it was. Lleu grew strong and whole again, and sought compensation for his suffering. He refused to accept the land, territory, silver, and gold which Goronwy offered as recompense. The material world and its goods, the shining pentacles of earth, no longer captivated Lleu, who had previously sought just such worldly solace in the comforts of the flesh and the acquisition of things. He killed Goronwy with a single thrust of his spear and continued to reign over his land prosperously thereafter. No more Mr. Nice Guy—the soft, overly accommodating Lleu had healed his own strength. This process of healing forced him to recognize and to *accept* his true inner nature, and to act in accordance with it. His slaying of the shadow within symbolizes his search for justice in the truest, most principled, most natural form imaginable. Lleu had integrated his feelings in the highest sense. He had become the knowing god, the eagle made whole, the Sun King and the shaman.[15]

93

The King must feel at home with *all* his earthly concerns—the ecology of the land as well as with business and politics. Nature, in all her wild glory, provides the King with the ultimate sounding board. It is a barometer which enables him to see just how far his personal weaknesses have led him astray. When the King's actions demonstrate a desire to align himself with Nature, he has become capable of making decisions that will transform his vulnerable, wounded self into a new self founded upon wholeness and strength. This process of transformation is like a dance whereby men mediate between the Shadow King and the Sun King, both of whom lie within us in a state of silent potentiality.

But what about the fierce emotions, the rages and tempests of the sea king? Lleu may slay Goronwy with a spear, but it is not so easy—nor so desirable—simply to *slay* our instincts. As we have seen, we need to set them dancing the dance of transformation. And in order to dance that dance, the King must draw upon the same primal source that sustains and informs the Magician: he must come to know the Wild Man. In time, as we shall see, the King must don the antlered crown and acknowledge himself as consort and son of the land he rules.

But if the King is vital to the maintenance of any society, he must sometimes sacrifice himself for the sake of the common good. The King must gain a more than passing familiarity with hell.

The silver serving platter in the Grail Castle is a conveyer of substance. But the question remains: is the substance which it holds food for the body, mind, or soul? If it feeds the body, then the animal nature will feel secure and be satisfied and nourished and thus made whole. If the substance borne upon the dish feeds the mind, then Perceval doesn't really need to ask questions—simply seeing the platter should provide him with enough mental information to satisfy his curiosity and logic. But if the dish carries food for the soul, Perceval will need to experience this through an inner sense of oneness, completion, and perfection. But Perceval only sees the dish in passing. He has not eaten of its substance, which in some versions of the Grail story is a fish, in another is connected with the blood which drips from the lance, and in the tale of "Peredur" in the *Mabinogion* is in fact a severed head which speaks prophecy![16] In any event, Perceval has not made this substance *his own*. So he cannot know, will not know, until he dares to journey farther into the ultimate silence. Since he has been so severely taken to task precisely for being silent, this would seem a mystical paradox at best!

The fish (a symbol of the Self), the blood, and the prophetic head all suggest that the mystical serving dish does in fact contain "soul food." This tells us that although the King rules over physical reality, he only rules *in truth* when he has seen a bit of the Otherworld and gained the ability to transcend physical reality at will. This is a journey which many contemporary Kings, tied to the concerns of the material world, are all too reluctant to make. It is a journey for which Perceval, in his first youthful visit to the Grail Castle, is not yet quite ready—thus proving that he is not yet a King.

For many (as it will be for Perceval), the journey to the Otherworld is a journey into silence. An episode of the television series *Northern Exposure* chronicles such a journey on the part of Chris, the local disc jockey, ex-con, and philosopher. Chris decides it is high time to go on a quest in the form of a spiritual retreat. He selects a monastery and arrives on his motorcycle (the vehicle which serves so many contemporary Warriors for the "snow-white charger" of Arthurian days). He is enthusiastic to perform acts of humility and abstinence. Much to his chagrin, he discovers that these monks live fairly high on the hog: they wear comfortable garments rather than scratchy sackcloth and enjoy wholesome gourmet cooking rather than living on kennel rations. It seems as if Chris will have little opportunity to make his Otherworld journey. He is assigned the chore of bee-keeping, and it is at the apiary that he meets a monk who embodies his idea of what a real monk should be. This is Brother Simon, who lives within his deep cowl in a state of absolute *silence*. Because Chris is a man of words, it is silence which touches off his own particular vision of the Otherworld. He can't stop *talking* about it—whether to the other monks, the unresponsive Brother Simon, or even to himself. Finally, he dreams about Brother Simon—and the dreams are sexual. He begins to fear that he has uncovered a buried homosexuality within himself. In extreme spiritual distress, he confesses to

Brother Simon. But Brother Simon turns out to be a she—a woman who chose the life of silence and obscurity among men in a monastery. So Chris uncovers his anima, his feeling self. In terms of Celtic myth, we are once again in the Castle of Damsels! Chris bravely forgs ahead in an endeavor to face himself and know himself, come what may. In the process he retrievs his soul.

At some time or another, every King must journey into the Otherworld—he must face himself, know himself, come what may. In one of the old Welsh poems, King Arthur stages a raid upon the Underworld realm of Annwn,[17] and in the more familiar medieval version of his story he is wounded unto death and carried on a magic barge to the Otherworldly isle of Avalon. The Lover matures into the Magician by virtue of such a shaman-quest, and this is how the Warrior matures into the King. Only men who are fully grown—who are men and not boys—can take the dark road across the "bridge of dread" and enter the Castle of Marvels without losing their souls. The Lover, as we have seen earlier, often makes the journey when he is too young and gets stuck there forever.

The Underworld journey often exacts a heavy price from the King. Because he lives a life which is dedicated to the land or the society as a whole, he may even become a kind of sacrifice to that land or society. We have seen how Lovers and Magicians met their end in the Neolithic. Later, in the Bronze Age, it appears to have been the King who was sacrificed, for the good of the land and the people. So the King must live a life which is impersonal. Hence his aching loneliness, his wound.

In medieval lore, it is the enchantress Morgan le Fay who comes with her death barge to bear the wounded King Arthur to the other side. This medieval lady of magic has strong pagan roots: she is none other than the Morrigan, the goddess who watches over and protects Cuchulain, greatest of Warriors. Her animal form is the raven, and—like her Norse sisters, the Valkyries—she gathers up the bodies of men slain on the battlefield. She is a bone collector, like the Hindu Kali or La Loba of Mexican folklore.[18] These bone goddesses particularly like to collect that which is in jeopardy of being lost forever, that which is endangered, crying out, dying out, going extinct. When all the bones are gathered and the missing

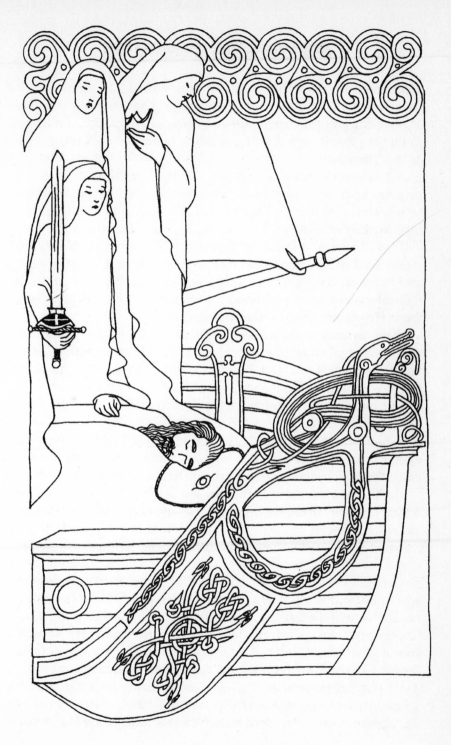

King Arthur Being Taken to Avalon

pieces set into place, the bone goddesses heal. The dead and the dying are made whole. Once again drawing breath, they open their eyes, rise up, laugh, dance, run away. Souls and spirits are returned to their rightful owners by these black-feathered cackling women of the Otherworld.

The death crones perpetuate the cycle of life. And in that process, no living being can escape death's ghostly specter. But to be reborn is also part and parcel of death. If we run, death is sure to follow us. If we vow to make a commitment, to remain quiet and still, to hold our ground, then death will find us in peace. And death itself will be nourished by our ability to trust, to stand ready and waiting for her with our eyes closed. Faith, confidence, reliance, acceptance, sureness, conviction, fidelity, loyalty—all of these virtues are food for the starving soul.

The wounded Fisher King suffers endlessly. He spends his days and nights in agony. He cannot walk. He cannot attend to his body, his people, his land. He does not die, does not know death, because he is afraid to live, to love *himself*.

He cannot sing. Neither can his lamed thighs dance the dance of transformation.

The Fisher King protects himself within the walls of the Grail Castle, surrounded by grandeur and sweet serving maids. He may go out to fish, but is he strong enough to eat what he catches?

In the spiritual sense, the answer is no. The fish of the Self which emerges from the ocean of the unconscious is still beyond his reach. He can only watch as life passes him by. And so he is doomed to live a death in life, not knowing that in death there is life anew.

Arthur must lose himself and be borne by the goddesses, wounded and sick, down to the Underworld. Here he will be healed, as will the land. Arthur will sleep, but he will come again. On the collective level, modern-day Americans clearly hope for such a renewal. It is interesting to note that we have to some degree projected this myth upon John F. Kennedy, the young King whose death was unconsciously perceived as a sacrifice for the nation as a whole. The scandal rags—which often show a remarkable predilection for enunciating modern archetypes—even insist that Kennedy, like Arthur, is living still, wounded and isolated, waiting to return to his people and renew the worldly Camelot. (The same news magazines also specialize in "Elvis sightings," testimony to yet another "king" waiting to come again.)

In order to heal ourselves—to renew our inner wasteland and perhaps even do our part to heal the collective wasteland around us—we must follow Perceval and other Celtic heroes on their Otherworld voyages. We will have to make the same journey Perceval made.

As Perceval returned older and wiser to the Grail Castle after many quests and adventures, so men, in the middle of their lives, must often seek a return to that consciousness of primal unity which we have defined as the grail experience.

Like Perceval, then, we shall return to the Grail Castle. We shall attempt to make our way through its mystical topography until we reach the center and gently lift the mask from the wounded sea king's face to see who the Fisherman really is.

Your inner King expresses itself positively if:

1. You are willing to undertake heroic journeys into unknown territory (foreign countries, new job skills, inner issues).

2. You exemplify exciting new ideals and philosophies of life among your social and/or business circle.

3. You can be both vulnerable and strong.

4. Preserving valuable traditions is important to you.

5. You obey the laws of the land and seek to embody civic virtues.

6. You have learned to acknowledge inner visions as a guiding force in your life.

7. You question the consensus views of authority and reality.

8. Bestowing generous favors is a pleasurable activity for you.

9. You are not afraid to construct a new identity based on the real you.

███████████████

10. You are willing to sacrifice yourself (i.e. your time and energy) for the sake of others.

Your inner King expresses itself negatively if:

1. You are overly ambitious, seeking to get all you can at the expense of others.

2. You isolate yourself rather than admit you are lonely.

3. You fear abandonment and death.

4. You believe that courage and heroic virtue are much more comfortably approached by way of your TV set.

5. You are secretly furious over the notion of women's empowerment.

6. You deny your own potential in order to remain part of the status quo.

7. Your house is on the hill, there are two cars in your garage, your wife is beautiful, your children are intelligent, you're highly successful—and you're still miserable.

8. The only wildlife you seek to protect is the stuff that's been growing on your unwashed dishes for a week.

9. You believe a man should be judged by the number and quality of his possessions.

10. You sometimes act in destructive, tyrannical, exploitative or abusive ways towards those who look up to you.

Notes

1. Robert Moore and Douglas Gillette, *The King Within: Accessing the King in the Male Psyche* (New York: William Morrow & Co., 1992), 59–62.

2. Gantz, *Mabinogion*, 84–5.

3. Ibid., 45–65.

4. Squire, *Celtic Myth and Legend*, 190–200.

5. Gantz, *Mabinogion*, 66–82.

6. Moore and Gillette, *The King Within*, 59–111.

7. MacCana, *Celtic Mythology*, 117.

8. Cited in Caitlin Matthews, *Arthur and the Sovereignty of Britain: King and Goddess in the Mabinogion* (London: Arkana, 1989), 23–4.

9. MacCana, *Celtic Mythology*, 117.

10. Cross and Slover, *Ancient Irish Tales*, 28–48.

11. Moore and Gillette, *The King Within*, 69–75.

12. New York: Dial Press, 1966.

13. Bly, *Iron John*, 98–113.

14. T.S. Eliot, "The Waste Land," in *The Waste Land and Other Poems* (New York: Harcourt, Brace & World, 1962), 42–3.

15. Gantz, *Mabinogion*, 115-7.

16. Ibid., 217–57.

17. Squire, *Celtic Myth and Legend*, 318–20.

18. Clarissa Pinkola Estes, *Women Who Run with the Wolves: Myths and Stories of the Wild Woman Archetype* (New York: Ballantine Books, 1992), 27–32.

CHAPTER 6

Discovering Your Archetypes

ere is a quiz to help you discover which male archetype plays the strongest role in your life. Perhaps you have already identified your principal archetype from previous chapters. However, the following quiz will enable you to focus on the various aspects of male psychology that are most active in your personality right now.

Be as honest as you can in answering the questions, so that you may ascertain which male mythological figures are strong in you and which ones are weak, repressed, or wounded. After all, transformation cannot occur until we are fully able to understand the true motivations and desires operative in the creation of our life experience.

Women may also take this test, answering each question in terms of the kinds of men to whom they are attracted. It may help them understand the basic archetype to which they resonate, and which very likely forms the principal component of their own animus or "man within."

Simply read the statements in each section and score according to *how much* or *how little* each statement applies to you. Circle the appropriate number indicated by the following numerical key:

3 = usually true
2 = moderately true
1 = rarely true
0 = almost never true

When you have completed the quiz, refer to the Male Archetype Scoring Columns at the end of the quiz to help you determine the mythic pattern which predominates in your life at this time.

Scoring

ONE: The World At Large

A. I believe it's still a man's world   3   2   1   0

B. I am actively involved in community affairs   3   2   1   0

C. I don't read the newspapers or watch TV—
I sense the world around me.   3   2   1   0

D. I study world events because I am fascinated
with information and new discoveries.   3   2   1   0

TWO: Reading Material

A. Politics, economics, and world history.   3   2   1   0

B. Psychology, New Age subjects, the frontiers
of science.   3   2   1   0

C. Poetry, fiction, entertainment, and the arts.   3   2   1   0

D. I seldom read anything except how-to manuals
or *Sports Illustrated*.   3   2   1   0

The Four Grail Treasures

THREE: Friends

A. I prefer the company of those who can help me elevate my position and status in life.   3 2 1 0

B. I have spiritual or intellectual friendships.   3 2 1 0

C. Most of my friends are women.   3 2 1 0

D. My friends are my working colleagues and high-school buddies.   3 2 1 0

FOUR: Social Events

A. I like to play the magnanimous host.   3 2 1 0

B. I'm uncomfortable at parties and often spend my time analyzing the other guests.   3 2 1 0

C. I present my sensual, "macho" side to other people as a matter of course.   3 2 1 0

D. I try to charm other people, and I remain very conscious of their enjoyment and welfare.   3 2 1 0

FIVE: Hobbies

A. I work hard and have no time for hobbies.   3 2 1 0

B. Philosophy, religion, science, lectures.   3 2 1 0

C. Sports, exercise, camping, hunting.   3 2 1 0

D. Museums, art galleries, the theater.   3 2 1 0

SIX: Children

A. I have no desire for children because I am immersed in my work and/or my path.   3 2 1 0

B. My children are an extension of myself.   3 2 1 0

C. I am fulfilled by my children; they carry on my family name.   3 2 1 0

D. I love my children and care about their emotional well-being.   3 2 1 0

SEVEN: Sex

A. Sex is essentially a mystical experience.   3 2 1 0

B. I respond to flattery.   3 2 1 0

C. Good sex is like a great work-out session at
the gym.   3 2 1 0

D. Sex is great, but romance is better.   3 2 1 0

EIGHT: Love and Commitment

A. A committed marriage enhances the safety and
well-being of my property and my children.   3 2 1 0

B. Love and commitment require a higher spiritual
dimension.   3 2 1 0

C. Love is all that matters.   3 2 1 0

D A marriage commitment is important for one's
social status.   3 2 1 0

NINE: Partners

A. I want a submissive partner whom I can defend.   3 2 1 0

B. I need a romantic, sexually exciting partner.   3 2 1 0

C. I need a partner who understands my need for
both privacy and mental stimulation.   3 2 1 0

D. I need a partner who complements my position
in the world.   3 2 1 0

TEN: Childhood

A. As a child, I loved to read and daydream of faraway lands.   3 2 1 0

B. As a child, I had imaginary playmates and created my own inner worlds.   3 2 1 0

C. I was the leader of all the childhood games I played with my friends.   3 2 1 0

D. As a child, I loved sports and the great outdoors.   3 2 1 0

ELEVEN: Food

A. I enjoy the atmosphere surrounding my meal as much as I enjoy the food itself.   3 2 1 0

B. I eat simply because it's necessary.   3 2 1 0

C. My table is a place of dignity and hospitality.   3 2 1 0

D. I am health-conscious and eat to stay fit.   3 2 1 0

TWELVE: Residence

A. My home is my castle.   3 2 1 0

B. I like comfort and aesthetic surroundings.   3 2 1 0

C. My home is functional; it is convenient to my work.   3 2 1 0

D. I need privacy and open spaces.   3 2 1 0

THIRTEEN: Physical Self

A. I pride myself on feeling active and fit.   3 2 1 0

B. I'm a touchy-feely sort of a guy.   3 2 1 0

C. I am physically shy, sometimes embarrassed by my body.   3 2 1 0

D. I often feel disconnected from my body.   3 2 1 0

FOURTEEN: Appearance

A. I dress for success, whether in a blue collar
   or white.   3 2 1 0

B. I am a very fashionable guy.   3 2 1 0

C. I am conservative in my attire.   3 2 1 0

D. My appearance is rather offbeat and eccentric.   3 2 1 0

Scoring: How to Determine
Your Dominant Male Archetype

On the scoring form on the following page, list each of your answers
for each question under the appropriate archetypal column. You will
find the four letters, A-D, arranged under the male archetypes they
represent.

Simply enter the number you circle for a particular statement
next to its letter, like this:

Warrior	Lover	Magician	King
1 = A _2_	1 = C _1_	1 = D _3_	1 = B _0_
2 = D _1_	2 = C _3_	2 = B _2_	2 = A _0_

Now add up the numbers for each male archetype column. The
male archetypes that are strong within you will have the highest
scores, and the weakest ones the low scores.

Male Archetype Scoring Columns

Warrior	Lover	Magician	King
1 = A ___	1 = C ___	1 = D ___	1 = B ___
2 = D ___	2 = C ___	2 = B ___	2 = A ___
3 = D ___	3 = C ___	3 = B ___	3 = A ___
4 = C ___	4 = D ___	4 = B ___	4 = A ___
5 = C ___	5 = D ___	5 = B ___	5 = A ___
6 = C ___	6 = D ___	6 = A ___	6 = B ___
7 = C ___	7 = D ___	7 = A ___	7 = B ___
8 = A ___	8 = C ___	8 = B ___	8 = D ___
9 = A ___	9 = B ___	9 = C ___	9 = D ___
10 = D ___	10 = A ___	10 = B ___	10 = C ___
11 = D ___	11 = A ___	11 = B ___	11 = C ___
12 = C ___	12 = B ___	12 = D ___	12 = A ___
13 = A ___	13 = B ___	13 = D ___	13 = C ___
14 = A ___	14 = B ___	14 = D ___	14 = C ___
Totals: ___	___	___	___

The following outline will further enhance your understanding of the predominant male archetype pervading your life. You may also wish to re-read the chapter about the archetype in which you achieved your highest (and lowest) score. If you scored almost equally high in two archetypes, then both patterns are powerful forces within you. The lowest score indicates the area where work is needed to strengthen, sublimate, or heal the personality.

If the Warrior is your archetype:
You are innovative, assertive, and courageous. Your will, motivation, and desire nature are strong. You are passionate and impulsive, forceful, active, and driven to succeed. The processes involved in transformation, regeneration, and sex are important to you. You can be compulsive and obsessed by a fear of death. A natural leader, you are often branded as a power-seeker. You may also have a tendency towards self-destructive action. When responding at your highest level of potential, you are a vital individual, capable of acting with purpose and authority in order to achieve your life's goals. Creative self-expression is one of your strengths; so is the pride you take in your children and your accomplishments.

Suitable occupations include police work, the military, manufacturing, metallurgy, medicine, research, or investigation. You may also find it fruitful to become involved in financial partnerships, salvage, or the professions involved with death and dying. The Warrior may be a dentist, doctor, firefighter, machinist, surgeon, welder, IRS agent, government spy, criminal lawyer, scientist, mortician, butcher, coroner, bill collector, detective, or insurance claims adjuster.

If the Lover is your archetype:
You are naturally kind and affectionate toward others, relationships being of primary importance in your life. Ever the creative artist, you value harmony, beauty, and peace above all else. Your surroundings must be aesthetically pleasing to you. You are sensitive and spiritually inclined, with an active imagination and an idealistic nature. There may be a tendency to succumb to the lures of drugs and alcohol, for you are sometimes confused or easily deceived. You can reach your highest potential by adopting a more structured and disciplined lifestyle. Your greatest pleasure comes through spiritual awakening and the artistry involved in creating beautiful forms and images for others to enjoy.

Suitable occupations involve art, comfort, beauty, the human voice, money, liquids, household service, home and family, real estate, social gatherings, mediation, and institutions. The Lover may well be a vocalist, innkeeper, concierge, commercial artist, or art dealer, chef, caterer, real estate agent, legal mediator, marriage counselor, interior decorator, diplomat, florist, arbitrator, photographer, or poet.

If the Magician is your archetype:
You enjoy communicating with others in order to exercise your strong logic and reasoning abilities. You are restless, curious, flexible, quick-witted, and diversified in your thoughts and actions. Your ability to discriminate between truth and flasehood is very pronounced. Some of you Magicians will be attracted to leading-edge technology, but all of you will be fascinated by any arena which allows you to express your independent, original, and liberated personality. Your nervous system may be delicate and you would be wise to become more health-conscious. Other shortcomings may include an overly analytical or critical attitude toward others. A rebellious nature often brings sudden changes in your circumstances. You may reach your highest level of achievement through humanitarian interests and service to others.

Suitable occupations include all areas of communication, any profession which requires detailed analysis, skilled crafts, health, medicine, and occultism or metaphysics as well as scientific technology. The Magician may often be found working as a travel agent, word processor, statistical analyst, naturopath, massage therapist, librarian, bookkeeper, chemist, civil servant, radio or television personality, psychologist, electrician, inventor, astrologer, or salesman.

If the King is your archetype:
You are a vital individual with an extremely paternal nature. Warm-hearted, loyal, noble and generous to a fault, you live to fulfill a single-pointed purpose in life. You are regal and gallant in your actions; consequently, you are generally recognized as an authority figure in your own area, or perhaps in many different areas. You have breadth of vision and an expansive mind. Your optimism and prosperity-oriented outlook will see you through many difficulties. You can be ambitious, responsible, and disciplined in your behavior. Sometimes your big ego and your longing for status get in the way of building successful long-term relation-

ships. There is a tendency towards excessive, extravagant activities when you are feeling depressed, fearful, inhibited, or insecure. You can reach your highest level of achievement through creative endeavor, adventurous travel (the archetypal quest), and positions which give full range to your vast leadership potential.

Suitable fields of occupation include the stock market, big business in general, the clergy, the law, foreign affairs, and universities. The king may be a film director, judge, entrepreneur, theologian, professor, attorney, corporate executive officer, politician, ambassador, architect, building contractor, or civil engineer.

The archetypes symbolized by the Four Grail Treasures represent the paths men walk upon as they begin their quests through the forest of life. If we are strong and wise, and if we know who we are, we may walk our chosen path with clarity, dignity, and grace. This is what being a hero is all about.

But each of these archetypes is incomplete in and of itself. Each one constitutes only one single portion of a fourfold entity, a Higher Self which is symbolized in many different ways in many different world traditions, and which in our own journey is symbolized by the mandala of the Grail Castle.

When we return to the Grail Castle—a return which typically takes place in the middle of our lives—we may find that it is time to seek the wholeness which lies at the center of the mandala, the wholeness of the Higher Self. We may find ourselves unable to go on following just *one* road. We must learn to use the sword and the lance, the grail and the dish, with equal skill.

The heart of the Grail Castle is the bed where the sick sea king, the wounded Fisher King, lies in his stillness.

Let us, then, take the Otherworld journey to the center of the Grail Castle and meet the Fisher King face to face.

Part Two

CHAPTER 7

The Land of Youth

Having reached his thirty-fifth year, the poet Dante experienced what we would now call the "mid-life crisis." He felt as if he had wandered into a dark forest and lost his road. He could not quite remember how he got there: "so was I immersed in sleep, when the true way I left behind."[1]

It is at this juncture, "midway the journey" of their lives, that men begin to ask hard questions. For some years now, they have been encased in their suits of armor, wielding their swords of discrimination. The time when they, like Arthur's knights, plunged into the forest "where the woods were thickest" may seem almost like a distant memory now. Battles have been lost and won.

Typically, modern men have begun the journey by entering their professions, playing the Warrior and forging ahead with sword in hand to make their mark in the world. They have come upon the Castle of Damsels, exchanged their swords for a cup and played the Lover; perhaps they have married and had children. Some have even held for a time the Magician's wand, creating or inventing or simply navigating through the waters of life with their intuition. And, if they are "successful," they have become Kings, viewing the world from suburban castles and participating in the life of the community.

Not all men have all these experiences, but nearly everyone has had some of them. Some may not consider themselves successful— quite the contrary. But many of these apparent differences in their life paths pale into insignificance when they are faced with the emptiness of middle life. The implement they have become accustomed to wield most of the time—be it the sword, the cup, the wand, or the dish— seems to weigh heavy in their hands. Their battles seem futile, their relationships inadequate. Their vaunted powers are as nothing in the scheme of the universe, and their inner kingdom lies waste.

Men slash their way through the forest, fight their battles, and come to a deep, dark hollow in the woods where, according to Dante, everything is "so harsh, dismal and wild" that even death is scarcely more bitter.

What is it, then, that fills men with such emptiness at the onset of midlife? What is the dark canyon in the center of men's hearts that makes them feel oppressed, bitter as death?

In order to answer that question, let us return to the childhood experience of the Grail Castle, that perfect moment we left behind near the end of Chapter 1. In our first examination, we established that the Grail Castle:

- Is a mandala or symbol of wholeness and mystical unity with all things

- That the experience of this wholeness or unity is also a psychological reality, one which all of us have undergone at one time or another

- That men must sacrifice this childlike sense of oneness with the universe in order to take up the sword of discrimination and walk one of the paths of manhood

- That the mystical experience of the Grail Castle returns to men thereafter only in fugitive moments of beauty— moments which make men seem temporarily "spaced out" but which leave them with a nostalgic longing for the Grail Castle experience

It is to satisfy this longing for the Grail Castle that men typically begin the search once again, in the middle of their lives. There are, of course, some who begin the search much earlier—these are the full-time questers, mystics, and spiritual wanderers for whom all things save the grail moment have always appeared to be a waste of time. And there are others who are unable to undertake the Grail Quest at all. They have wielded their swords with too heavy a hand, and cannot put them down. They are now unwilling or unable to look within themselves, leave the fast lane behind, or emerge from their self-imposed walls, their suits of armor. These unfortunate men are the ones who suffer heart attacks at the early age of forty or forty-five.

Therefore, it matters little how old a man is in actuality—whether his Grail Quest is a lifelong affair, the crest of a mid-life crisis, or a belated attempt to save part of his soul. The essential question is:

How shall we emerge from our castle walls? How shall we find the Grail Castle once again?

It will do us little good to return to our original story, the *Perceval* of Chretien de Troyes. Chretien's book was never finished: the author died as Perceval was still wandering through the woods, meeting adventure after adventure. Several other writers tried to complete Chretien's poem; each writer found his own separate path back to the Grail Castle. In fact, all the writers who took up the Grail story during the Middle Ages appear to have sought their own individual roads to the Fisher King's sorrowful kingdom. We shall have occasion to follow a few of them through the forest later on.

But perhaps the best way to find a path through this particular stretch of the woods is to tap the original source. The reader may remember that we compared the Grail journey to a kind of "vision quest" and hinted that it has its origins in stories about the journeys of Celtic heroes to the Otherworld, Tir-na-nog, the "Land of Youth."

Scholars have, in fact, long been aware that the medieval Grail stories appear to be descendants of an old Celtic literary genre called *echtrae*, meaning "adventures"—although the reference here is to adventures in the Otherworld rather than in this one.

Let us, then, follow some of the heroes of Celtic myth on their journeys to the Land of the Living.

Before a man can enter the Otherworld, he must receive the call. A guide must come to him, an emissary from the Land of Youth, and conduct him through the psychic gateways that will lead him beyond the bounds of ordinary reality. Sometimes the guide is a man like himself, a warrior from the beyond. King Cormac was standing on Tara's ramparts when he saw a man approaching, a "calm, gray-haired warrior," marvelously dressed, who carried with him "a branch of silver with three golden apples." So wondrous was the music made by this branch that all the folk of Tara wondered where the man had come from.

"From a land wherein there is naught save truth," said the warrior, "and there is neither age nor decay nor gloom nor sadness nor envy nor jealousy nor hatred nor haughtiness."

Cormac greatly desired the magical silver branch and thus sought to form an alliance with the mysterious warrior. But the warrior was only willing to sacrifice the branch in exchange for three gifts (one for each golden apple) from Cormac. The king agreed, though much to his sorrow, for the warrior returned three times, successively carrying off Cormac's daughter, son, and wife. It was after the third time that Cormac himself took horse and followed the warrior to the Otherworld.[3]

Sometimes it is an animal which leads the hero to the Otherworld. The great warrior Cuchulain (see Chapter 2) was attending a Samhain Feast. Samhain is the old Celtic equivalent of our Halloween, the day when the gateways to the Otherworld stand open. To please his wife, he cast his spear at two magic swans which appeared flying through the sky. He failed to bring down the birds, but their magic cast a spell over him. Cuchulain fell into a visionary sleep which lasted for a year, until Samhain came again and he journeyed to the Otherworld. We may also remember that Pwyll, Prince of Dyved, made an Otherworld journey to fight on behalf of the

Goddess (Chapter 3). He was out hunting when a stag raced by him. His hounds took off in pursuit of the stag, and Pwyll followed, in pursuit of the hounds. Soon there was yet another pack of hounds in pursuit, and these animals were white with red ears. It was in following these spectral hounds that Pwyll encountered their owner, Arawn, King of the Otherworld, waiting for him in a clearing.

The magic stag is a feature of later Arthurian stories as well. After Chretien de Troyes died with his *Perceval* still unfinished, the poem was continued by a writer named Gautier, who brought Perceval to a mysterious castle where he won himself an even more mysterious lover called the Red Star Woman. Here we are at the Castle of Damsels once again! As medieval ladies were prone to do, the Red Star Woman set Perceval a task—to take a white hound and hunt a white stag. Perceval hunted and killed the stag, but was then confronted with its owner, a sinister and angry woman who led him into even stranger realms of magic.

It is difficult to extract original mythic themes from medieval romances, but we may suspect that the Castle of Damsels is the portal to the Otherworld, and that Perceval has encountered the Goddess in her positive aspect (Red Star Woman), and in her more chthonic or destructive guise as well (the angry woman). More important for our purposes is the fact that it is sometimes a magical animal which leads us to the Otherworld. Is this a way of saying that we must touch our own wildness, our animal selves, our primal and primitive nature, before we can enter upon the transformative journey? We are reminded of Gawain's visit to the Otherworld as recorded in *Sir Gawain and the Green Knight*. Does the ragged wild man, gigantic and dressed all in green, represent such a primal force?

As fascinating as these questions are, we must leave them for a later chapter. At present, we are concerned with the Otherworld journey itself; we must wait a bit to unravel all the mysteries that lie therein.

And it is time now to encounter the most common of all Otherworldly guides, for warrior, stag and swan are less often met with at the initial stages of the journey than is the shining, magical Woman of Faerie who beckons men to follow her into the Land of the Living.

Perhaps the finest example of this sort of Otherworld call may be found in "The Adventure of Bran"—who is an altogether different Bran than the kingly son of Llyr. According to the story, Bran was walking near his home when he heard a strange sweet music behind him. Though he turned round and round, the music always seemed to be yet behind him. Like Cuchulain, he fell into a trance-like sleep, and when he awoke he found beside him a silver branch with white flowers—which is almost certainly the same branch as that presented to King Cormac by the "calm, gray-haired warrior" from the Otherworld. Bran took the silver branch home with him, and there appeared before all those assembled in the hall a beautiful woman, strangely garbed, who sang to them of the joys of the Otherworld. The woman vanished, and Bran set sail across the sea next day, in search of the Land of Youth.

Connla the Fair underwent an almost identical experience. He was standing on the hill of Usnach when he saw a woman in "unfamiliar dress." She said to him:

"I come from the Lands of the Living, where there is neither death nor want nor sin. We keep perpetual feast without need for service. Peace reigns among us without strife. A great fairy-mound it is, in which we live; wherefore we are called 'folk of the fairy-mound.'"[4]

Connla's companions are somewhat distressed over his dialogue with a woman whom they themselves can neither see nor hear. One of the court Druids drives her away with a spell—but not before she tosses an apple to Connla. This must be yet one more of the Otherworldly apples on the silver branch which the gray-haired warrior bestowed upon Cormac, corresponding to the white flowers on the branch which came to Bran. In any event, it put Connla in a sulk. He could take no food or drink save the apple itself, which was always renewed as soon as he consumed it. Finally, unable to bear the realms of mortals any longer, he encountered the mysterious woman once again and set sail with her for the Land of Youth.

We have seen how Pwyll, the hero of the *Mabinogion*'s First Branch, followed the hounds of Arawn to a magical encounter with the Otherworld lord. This was not his only journey to the

The Faery Feast

fairy realms. We may also remember how he pursued the beautiful Rhiannon on a moonlight ride, as she rode a magic steed which always eluded him. Was Rhiannon yet another Otherworld maiden, calling the hero to undertake the magic journey?

Almost certainly she was. Pwyll was sitting on a fairy mound, in hopes of "seeing a wonder," when she appeared to him. She asked him to come and rescue her at the court of her father, Heveydd the Ancient, and we may agree with the majority of scholars who see in Heveydd's court yet another portrait of the Otherworld.

Sometimes a man may receive the call from his inner Warrior, the heroic guide of the soul who is always within him, no matter how far he has strayed from his own Warrior path. Sometimes he receives the call from a swan or a stag, or perhaps from the Wild Man within, all of which indicate his most primal, animal instincts. Most often it is the anima, the woman within, his own female soul, who calls him.

And then he falls asleep—or so it seems. Cuchulain languished in sleep for a year, Bran fell asleep outside his home, and Connla went into a deep sulk.

It is during this trance or sleep that the hero begins his journey to the Otherworld. Sometimes he travels by land, sometimes by sea. King Cormac pursued the gray-haired warrior across a plain. He rode into a mist and became separated from all his companions. It was in that mist that he came upon the house of the Otherworld. Similarly, Pwyll of Dyved rode into the realms of Arawn, and it was after a long ride through grim country that Sir Gawain chanced upon the mysterious castle which housed the lord, the lady, and old Morgan le Fay.

This idea of the Otherworld as a land which lies just beyond the reaches of the ordinary landscape, in a dimension only slightly removed from our own, perhaps inside one of the old Neolithic barrow mounds which dot the Celtic landscape, is a common one. In Ireland, the barrow mounds are the "hills" of the *ben sidhe* or "people of the hills," and these "people of the hills" are none other than the old gods, the Tuatha de Danaan. It is written that after the gods departed from earth, leaving the place to mere mortals, they took up residence in the various barrow mounds, and in fact numerous barrows in Ireland are regarded as the home of specific deities. The most famous example is that of the great Neolithic tomb called Newgrange, reputedly the home of Angus mac Og (see Chapter 3). We may remember the words of the Otherworldly woman who visited Connla the Fair, as noted above: "A great fairy-mound it is, in which we live; wherefore we are called 'folk of the fairy-mound.'" Clearly, then, Connla is journeying to the land of the gods. During Cuchulain's trance-like sickness, his charioteer made the Otherworld journey in his stead and reported back: "There is a well in that noble palace of the fairy-mound."

This Otherworld tradition has survived in British and Irish folk-lore in the form of tales about men who visit "the barrow mounds." An individual typically finds himself lost—perhaps in a mist, as in so many of the older tales—and somehow finds himself inside one of the old barrow mounds. There he encounters a band of happy, shining people who invite him to a feast. But alas for the unwary traveler who eats of that food or drinks of that drink! For after the party is over and he finds himself outside again, he usually discovers that many years have passed while he feasted inside the fairy realm.

Sometimes, however, the Land of Youth is perceived as an isle in the West. Connla the Fair set sail in a coracle to find the Other-world, and so did Bran. In the tale of Bran's voyage, the woman from the Otherworld sings of an entire archipelago, lying in the most distant West:

> There are thrice fifty distant isles
> In the ocean to the west of us;
> Larger than Erin twice
> Is each of them, or thrice.[5]

The story of Cuchulain's Otherworld voyage, however, con-tains a journey in which both concepts are linked. Cuchulain's charioteer travels across the magic plain in a chariot, then across a lake in a boat of bronze bound for a magic isle.

The Otherworld itself is no dark land of shades or unhappy ghosts, as was the Greek Hades. The Celtic Land of Youth is more akin to the Elysian Fields of Greek myth, a happy land where dead heroes wandered in a kind of supernal bliss. In fact, the Celtic Otherworld has its own specific geography. Those who sail there across the waters come to:

> *… a distant isle,*
> *Around which sea-horses glisten:*
> *A fair course against the white-swelling surge,—*
> *Four pillars uphold it. …*
>
> *A beauty of a wondrous land,*
> *Whose aspects are lovely,*
> *Whose view is a fair country,*
> *Incomparable is its haze.*
>
> *Then if Silvery Land is seen,*
> *On which dragon-stones and crystals drop,*
> *The sea washes the wave against the land,*
> *Hair of crystal drops from its mane. …*
>
> *It is a day of lasting weather*
> *That showers silver on the lands,*
> *A pure-white cliff on the range of the sea,*
> *Which from the sun receives its heat.*[6]

This, according to the song of the Otherworldly woman in the tale of Bran's voyage, is what it looks like—the first glorious sighting of the Land of Youth. It is a vision which still lies within all of us, and which finds its resonance in more modern tales as well:

> *And the ship went out into the High Sea and passed on into the West, until at last on a night of rain Frodo smelled a sweet fragrance on the air and heard the sound of singing that came over the water. And then it seemed to him that as in his dream in the house of Bombadil, the grey rain-curtain turned all to silver glass and was rolled*

*back, and he beheld white shores and beyond them a far
green country under a swift sunrise.*[7]

Sometimes the Otherworld traveler is greeted just before his
arrival by none other than Manannan mac Lir, the Irish sea god
who, after the gods had departed from the earth, became the king
of Tir-na-nog. In Bran's tale, Manannan comes riding over the
waves in a chariot to greet the voyagers.

Sometimes, however, the male journeyer is met by bands of fair
women, whom we may suspect are none other than the inhabitants
of Morgan Le Fay's Avalon or the Castle of Damsels. The "Otherworld Song" of Bran's tale goes on as follows:

> *If he has heard the voice of the music,*
> *The chorus of the little birds from Imchiuin,*
> *A small band of women will come from a height*
> *To the plain of sport in which he is. ...*
>
> *Do not fall on a bed of sloth,*
> *Let not thy intoxication overcome thee;*
> *Begin a voyage across the clear sea,*
> *If perchance thou mayst reach the land of women.*[8]

"If he has heard the voice of the music, the chorus of the little
birds..." So runs the song. The birds who sing so beautifully are, in
fact, the birds of the goddess Rhiannon, and so they are called in
the old Welsh poems. The heroes who bore the severed head of
King Bran (the Bran of the *Mabinogion,* not the Otherworldly voyager) back to Wales feasted for years in a magic hall, lulled by the
singing of those same birds. There were three of these magic birds,
just as there were three apples on the branches brought to Cormac
and Connla, or three flowers on the branch which made such sweet
music for the voyager Bran. For the Otherworld woman is none
other than Rhiannon, and it is her music that is heard by the seeker
of the Land of Youth.

All men have heard the Otherworldly music at one time or
another in their lives. This experience is, in fact, much the same as

the Grail Castle experience we described earlier. The Otherworldly music, the singing of Rhiannon's birds, is the music of the infinite which draws men into that state of mystic unity which is the Grail Castle. It is the music that great composers hear within their souls, and place upon the page. It is the music poets hear and transcribe into "winged words." When men create—when they function as artists or bards who speak the great truths of the human soul—they are, in fact, just listening to the music of the Land of Youth.

It is Rhiannon who sings the song. For every man, be he Warrior, Lover, Magician, or King, there is a feminine image which sleeps beneath the surface of his waking mind. She comes in dreams; she makes herself manifest through poems and songs. Jungian psychologists call her the anima, and medieval men called her the "lady soul." For the unconscious of a man is a female thing, his lady soul indeed. She is the Beatrice or Rhiannon who comes forth from a man's very depths to lead him into the deeply unconscious realm of the Grail Castle, the Land of Youth. Only she can rightly guide him, for this is her realm. This is where she dwells. Thus it is the feminine spirit, the enchantress whose name, throughout history, has been Morgan Le Fay, Nimue, or Beatrice, who leads a man on, across the sea of the spirit, to the fair land which is the Self within.

Jung once said that it is a man's burden to live a life of discrimination, of isolation, and a woman's burden always to seek relationship. A man's lady soul is "related" in the deepest possible way, for she lives in the Grail World where everything is unity. Now we can see why the Land of Youth—at least as far as men are concerned—is a Castle of Damsels, a land of women. Let men study their dreams; they may upon occasion find themselves in a house inhabited by many women, or by one numinous and glorious woman. Such dreams are of great importance, for they symbolize our journey to the Castle of Damsels.

Now we can see why the Lover is also the artist. For him, the anima is close to the surface of consciousness. She is so close that he can almost touch her, hold her in his arms. In fact, he really *does* hold her in his arms whenever he exercises his remarkable creative talents. But alas, sometimes Rhiannon draws a bit *too* close to her chosen Lovers. These men see the anima everywhere—and especially in the faces of the women who enter their own lives. Poor Lover, in love not with a real woman but with Rhiannon, reflection of his own soul! Poor woman, forced to take on the burden of the Goddess instead of being appreciated for herself! The Warrior, locked in his suit of armor, finds it much more difficult to meet the Goddess, and yet he cannot become a King unless he learns to meet her, to make the Otherworld journey. Only the Magician really understands how to journey in and out of the Goddess's realm without falling victim to her charms. Only he is the master of the Otherworld voyage.

Though the Otherworldly music is most often the voice of the Goddess or her magic birds, it is sometimes an integral part of the land itself. As Bran the Voyager approached the Land of Youth, he and his men saw a wonder:

> Then they row to the conspicuous stone,
> From which arise a hundred strains.
>
> It sings a strain unto the host
> Through long ages, it is not sad,
> Its music swells with choruses of hundreds—
> They look for neither decay nor death.[9]

We may be reminded, and rightly so, of the stone which cried out when a king placed his foot upon it. We may also be reminded, and again quite rightly, of the standing stones of the British Isles. But this singing stone is a metaphor for something even more powerful and far-reaching: we have arrived at the very center of the universe.

Most traditional peoples honor the center of all things. This cosmic center is both the center of the world and the center of each mortal human being. It is the World Tree up which shamans climb on their journey to the land of the gods, the tree the ancient Norse called Yggdrasil. It is the World Mountain, Olympus or Mount Meru. Within the human body, it is the axis of the spinal column. This world axis leads upward, ever upward, to the North Star round which the universe revolves. And it is everywhere. Each tree, each stone, each smokehole in a shaman's hut from which the North Star may be seen, each spinal axis within each and every human being, is the center of the world. And in the center of all things, there is singing.

The world axis, whether stone or tree, forms the central core of the Otherworld. Though Bran the Voyager may have seen it as a singing stone in one part of the tale, he had already heard it described (by the Otherworld Woman) as a singing tree:

> *An ancient tree there is with blossoms,*
> *On which birds call the canonical Hours.*
> *'Tis in harmony it is their wont*
> *To call together every Hour.*[10]

We have, of course, reached rather peculiar territory indeed when Rhiannon's birds sing the Catholic hours in a pagan Otherworld! The Irish poems, though older than Christianity, were not written down until the early Middle Ages, when Irish monks still remembered their ancient traditions with love and delight, but felt compelled to cover their tracks in regard to the new faith. An older description of the World Tree may be found in the tale of Cuchulain's Otherworld journey:

> *At the entrance to the enclosure is a tree*
> *From whose branches there comes beautiful and harmo-*
> *   nious music.*
> *It is a tree of silver, which the sun illumines;*
> *It glistens like gold.*
>
> *There are thrice fifty trees.*
> *At times their leaves mingle, at times, not.*
> *Each tree feeds three hundred people*
> *With abundant food, without rind.*
>
> *There is a well in that noble palace of the fairy-mound.*
> *There you will find thrice fifty splendid cloaks,*
> *With a brooch of shining gold*
> *To fasten each of the cloaks.*[11]

The World Tree is a great hazel tree, yet also a tree of silver and gold. It is both one tree and many—a hundred and fifty, according to the poem. When Cormac emerged from his journey across the Plain of Mist and beheld the Otherworld, he too saw the World Tree. And the well which Cuchulain's charioteer saw "in that noble palace of the fairy-mound" was perceived by Cormac as five crystal streams:

> Then he saw in the enclosure a shining fountain, with five streams flowing out of it, and the hosts in turn drinking its water. Nine hazels of Buan grew over the well. The purple hazels dropped their nuts into the fountain, and the five salmon which were in the fountain severed them and sent their husks floating down the streams. Now the sound of the falling of those streams was more melodious than any music that men sing.[12]

Beyond the white-silver plain where the World Tree rises in its glory and the crystal streams flow forth, there stands the palace of the Otherworld king. But before we are quite ready to travel there, we must first understand a little bit more about where we are actually going.

Notes

1. Laurence Binyon, trans., "The Divine Comedy," in *The Portable Dante*, ed. Paolo Milano (New York: Viking Press, 1967), 3–4.

2. Ibid., 3.

3. Cross and Slover, *Ancient Irish Tales*, 503–4.

4. Ibid., 488.

5. Ibid., 591.

6. Ibid.

7. J.R.R. Tolkien, *The Return of the King* (New York: Ballantine, 1974), 384.

8. Cross and Slover, op. cit., 591.

9. Ibid., 590.

10. Ibid., 589.

11. Ibid., 189.

12. Ibid., 505.

CHAPTER 8

Ancient Journeys

What precisely is the Otherworld? If we take a very narrow, scholarly view of the subject, we might simply say that it is the Celtic "land of the dead," and nothing more. But such an answer is much too simple, even though it is true that there are good archaeological reasons to think of the Land of Youth as a world of the departed. Even before the Celts reached Western Europe, the megalith builders buried their dead facing west, toward the sunset and the great ocean. Judging from these westward-facing remains in Neolithic tombs as well as the considerable body of Celtic lore concerning the "drowned lands" in the West and the isle of Avalon set in its mist-enshrouded lake, the concept of the Otherworld as a Western Isle seems to have been the most ancient one. It was across this ocean that many Celtic heroes later journeyed in search of the Land of Youth.

To the megalith builders, this land across the sea was not so much a land of the dead as a "land of life." The skeletons inside megalithic tombs are often painted with red ocher, for red was the color of life, of vitality. The religion of the megalith builders seems never to have died out completely in the British Isles; the Celts who came afterwards retained a more powerful vision of the Otherworld than any other European people.

But if the Celtic Otherworld echoes that of the megalith builders who went before them, then who exactly built the megaliths?

The megalithic sites such as Stonehenge, Avebury, and Carnac which abound throughout the British Isles and France were built by aboriginal peoples who inhabited Western Europe long before the Celts. We do not know what they called themselves; folklorists and fantasy novelists alike sometimes refer to them as the Prytani, although it might be more correct simply to call them the Old Ones. They buried their dead in mounds of earth and stones called barrows, and the earliest of these megalithic tombs, located in France, go back to c. 3,500 BC. The Old Ones are usually described as "Neolithic," meaning that they lived in the "New Stone Age," an era characterized by farming villages. Their earliest weapons were slender arrows with delicate flint tips which resembled the shape of an elder leaf (the elder remained a magical tree into Celtic times, when it was considered sacred by the Druids).

The rituals of the Old Ones or Prytani were probably conducted inside the great stone circles they erected, and which are reminiscent of the magic circles found in shamanic rites all over the world. Many of the stone circles are oriented towards the solstice and equinox points or the risings of planets and stars, from which we may infer that their religion was in part based upon the worship of the stars, even as it was based upon the Great Mother as Goddess of Death and Rebirth.[1]

The Prytani were driven into the hinterlands of the British Isles by invading Indo-European tribes, among whom were the Celts. Some, however, believe that the Old Ones may have influenced the development of Druidic thought. By the beginning of the Christian era, most of the Old Ones had probably retreated to Cornwall and Wales, or to northerly regions like Perth and Argyll. One can still see vestiges of the Prytanic bloodline running through the current inhabitants of these regions, as well as among the people commonly called "black Irish." It is said in legend that Merlin was the son of a

A Druid/Shaman

mortal woman and an imp, elf, or devil—which may simply record an old belief that Merlin himself had a Prytanic heritage.[2]

By Christian times, these aboriginal inhabitants of Britain had been almost entirely forgotten. Contemporary writers of "high fantasy" have romanticized them as elves, fairies, or descendants of lost Atlantis. Until quite recently, rural Celtic people believed (and perhaps still do) that the Old Ones had returned to the heath, to the earthworks, forts, and barrows which they themselves erected. Such sites have traditionally been regarded as doorways to the Otherworld, and it is said[3] that on Lammas (August 2) and Hollandtide (November 11) the barrows often sparkle and blaze at night as with the light of many stars, shape-shifting, moving about the landscape, appearing first in one place, then another.

These man-made hills which contain the bones of the dead rise up on the sea of great open plains. Some of them resemble the earthen breasts of the old Mother Goddess, or perhaps a female form swollen with child. Indeed, some of the barrows, such as Wimble Toot (i.e. teat), appear to have been named to convey precisely that impression. Certain mountains, such as the Paps of Anu in Ireland (Anu being simply a short form of Danu, goddess mother of the old Irish deities or Tuatha de Danaan), seem to have a similar history.[4]

Before being returned to the Earth Mother and buried in the stone chambers, the skeletons of the Prytani were painted red, symbolizing life and vitality. Thus the goddess would know that such an individual was to be reconstituted, brought back to life.

The bodies of the dead may have been laid out on high rocky cliffs or hung in trees (a common practice among Native American tribes), or sometimes placed in special open pits, so that the ravens, hawks, eagles, and elements could pick the bones clean and chalky white. This work of rendering the human form to bone and then reconstituting or resurrecting it was the work of that universal figure of shamanic religions, the Old Bone Goddess. In later times the Celts knew her as the Morrigan or Raven Woman, ancestress of the medieval enchantress Morgan le Fay. The Norse recognized a whole troop of such bone collectors, the Valkyries. It was the Bone Goddess who picked over the remains of slain warriors, a work which can only be accomplished by she who knows the wild, free essence of the soul, the instinctive life, the deepest of all knowing. In shamanic rituals the world over, the bones of the dead are collected, preserved, and assembled, then thought, sung, and shaken back to life. In old versions of the Cinderella fairy tale, the heroine sings a song over the bones of her favorite household critter and it is this reconstructed totem, rather than a fairy godmother, who delivers the goods. By such tortuous cultural paths have Disney cartoons evolved from the primordial Bone Mother.

The goddess as life-giver or rejuvenator was known to the Celts as Madron, who dwelt among the shadows of Annwn, or as Rhiannon, with her three faces: the maiden who lures Pwyll away from his kingdom at the fairy mound of Arberth, the mother who gives herself to the lord of the Otherworld in exchange for the safe return of her son Pryderi, and the widowed crone who accepts Manawyddan as her husband to keep him from grieving for his brothers and companions, the slain sons of Llyr.

During the journey to the Otherworld, a soul which has been lost to itself is breathed back into the body, its livingness restored. The Prytani had their ways of conducting the living through these cycles of death and rebirth. Magical rites, sports, and games are still performed on barrow mounds today, to raise energy from the earth up into the body, a way of refilling a cup that has been emptied.[5] The magister or guiding spirit of such rites, the ancestor of all latter-day magicians, was the shaman.

We have already mentioned the shaman in our description of Celtic Otherworld journeys. Indeed, many of the adventures of Celtic voyagers to the Land of Youth seem to echo the archetypal journey of the shaman. And if the journey to the Grail Castle is in fact based on earlier voyages to the Otherworld, then we may say that every man is, in a sense, a shaman when he takes the road back to the Grail Castle.

The word shaman is of Siberian origin and refers to a religious specialist—we sometimes call him a "medicine man"—who journeys to the Otherworld in the service of his people or tribe. As part of his initiation, a Siberian shaman typically experiences a vision in which he is reduced to a skeleton. The Bone Goddess or Lady of

Wild Beasts then collects the bones, sings a song over them, and brings him back to life.

Having experienced his initiatory death and rebirth, the shaman is ready to devote his life to his people. He seeks visions for them. Some of these visions, like that of the nineteenth-century Lakota shaman Black Elk, still have resonance for the people a hundred and fifty years later. To begin his quest for the redeeming wisdom, the shaman beats a drum, then slips into a trance. Taking the form of his animal totem, which is often a bird (usually a swan among the ancient Celts), he journeys up the trunk of the World Tree, the tree which stands at the center of the world, and which we saw imaged as both tree and stone in the tale of Bran's voyage. The shaman thus reaches the land of the gods, the Grail Castle. Here he receives messages which will heal the tribe—just as we, in the stormy visions which characterize the dark center of our lives, may receive the inspiration which will make us genuine kings, caring for and healing the society in which we live.

The nature of the shaman's journey tells us something about the real identity of the Otherworld. It is synonymous with that other dimension which mystics and occultists have called the astral plane. This is the dimension of reality where most magical work is done, and ancient occult texts have always lavished great details on "maps" of the astral. The *Tibetan Book of the Dead* constitutes one such map; so does the *Egyptian Book of the Dead*. Kabbalistic magicians recognize their own elaborate geography of the astral plane, and, as we have seen, so did the ancient Celts.

The astral plane is a sacred space wherein one may divine great truths and heal oneself accordingly. It is not precisely separate from our physical world; it is, in fact, closely linked to it, a kind of reflection. Shadowy spirits and ghostly forms exist side by side with the verdant green foliage and earthy red clay of physical reality.

Dion Fortune, the renowned British occult writer of the early twentieth century, called the astral plane "the plane of illusion."[6] This is because there is no *form* on the astral plane, only *force*. Thus we may attribute powers such as mental telepathy or personal magnetism to the astral plane, as well as qualities such as our instincts, desires, and emotions. The unconscious mind is the interior landscape of the astral plane, serving as a mirror and a reflector for the intensity of our rational interpretations about life on this (seemingly) more tangible earth plane. This subjective aspect of consciousness, the place where dreams and creative deductions are made and brought through to fruition, is also a receptive medium for the energy which—according to Kabbalists, Hermeticists, and other seekers after magical illumination—flows down to us from still higher or more spiritual worlds. Whatever image or reality we may wish to create in the imagination, when ensouled with sufficient emotion, will, and desire, can eventually filter down and be made manifest on the physical plane, our ordinary reality.

Though psychologists insist that dreams are the language of the unconscious, a magician—or an old Celtic Druid—would probably have had a somewhat more far-reaching point of view. According to most workers in magic, the astral plane or Otherworld is where we go during sleep, when the mind disconnects from the physical senses. The Otherworld comes vividly to life when we are able to roam freely through the landscape of dreams. Sometimes we may endure nightmares or exaggerated tremors of emotion. This is because the astral plane serves to unleash our animal nature, wild, natural, free, and untamed, capable of producing psychic phenomena that confuse or deceive our more rational sense of things. This is why magicians and occultists have always considered the astral journey just as treacherous as it is rewarding; it is important that we attain mastery and harmony on the earth plane before we set off wandering in astral realms. On the psychological level, Perceval had to sacrifice the unitive world of childhood, so filled with feeling tones and emotional affect, in order to take the path of masculine discrimination. Only when he had learned to wield his sword properly would he be able to return to the Grail Castle—that midlife journey into the Self with which we are presently concerned. Taking a slightly different point of view—what we may call the magical point of view—we may say that Perceval had to master the world of reality before he could successfully take the shaman's journey into Otherworldly realms. For it is only when that passionate animal nature is mastered and trained, when we know what manner of creature we are, that we may be empowered by the force within us, whether we conceive of it as a god, an animal totem, or simply the power of the Self. Then the dream, the astral soul-walk, becomes a shaman's quest in the waking world.

The unconscious has deep recesses which plunge many fathoms down. These deeper holds of instinctual psychic knowledge contain the fund of memories and experiences of all humanity. It is this level of consciousness which Carl Jung named the collective unconscious, and which occultists have called the akashic records. This most fundamental level of human consciousness is the substance of the Otherworld, and it is in, from, and through this Otherworld substance that we have been formed. Through it we may be recollected (or re-collected), reconstituted, regenerated, and reconciled with our innermost Self.

The Land of Youth may sometimes be imagined as a place beyond the sea, sometimes just a wide plain beyond the mists which lie on the boundaries of home. Sometimes it is found within the old barrow mounds themselves, where the Tuatha de Danaan, the Celtic gods who brought the Grail Treasures to Ireland, are living yet. Wherever it may be, Celtic heroes journeyed there again and again, whether in body or in spirit. And the adventures they met with were less like visits to the dead than they were like rites of renewal; one returns from the Otherworld with a new sense of vision, of power. It is this aspect of the Otherworld journey—its initiatory or transformative power—with which we are concerned here. This is why we regard the Land of Youth, like the Grail Castle, as a state of consciousness, another dimension of psychic or spiritual reality—a region of wholeness within the human psyche which brings us to a consciousness of our own inner wholeness. This state of consciousness has its own rules, its own landscape and geography.

Thoughts of this internal Otherworld stir the imagination, incite the feelings, and arouse the deeper essences of the soul. When we have occasion to enter into it, we slip through the cracks in linear time and space. We begin a journey into what one might call the fourth dimension, the Twilight Zone, that musty wardrobe in the attic bedroom made famous by C.S. Lewis in his *Narnia Chronicles*—

a place where use of the famous *Star Trek* catch-phrase "Beam me up, Scotty" is applicable or sometimes even necessary. The Otherworld can be any place unfamiliar and unknown, where strange, wonderful, and oftimes frightening happenings abound. Thus the Otherworld remains as alive and well for citizens of the modern world as it always was for the Celts and other ancient peoples.

It is to this shining, misty region of the soul that we must journey if we are to find all the Grail Treasures and become whole, rather than remaining cast in a particular archetypal role, playing out the same dramas over and over again with the same empty motions.

Notes

1. Aubrey Burl, *Stone Circles of the British Isles*, passim.

2. For Neolithic Britain, see Jill Paton Walsh, *The Island Sunrise: Prehistoric Culture in the British Isles* (New York: Seabury Press, 1976); and Aubrey Burl, op. cit. For folklore and tradition concerning these early settlers, see Paul Huson, *Mastering Witchcraft* (New York: Berkley Windhover, 1970), 13–4.

3. Brian Frond and Alan Lee, *Faeries* (New York, Toronto, London: Peacock Press/Bantam Books, 1978).

4. Janet and Colin Bord, *Earth Rites: Fertility Practices in Pre-Industrial Britain* (St Albans: Paladin Books/Granada Publishing, 1982), 5.

5. Ibid., passim.

6. Dion Fortune, *Aspects of Occultism* (New York, Samuel Weiser, 1979), 27–33.

CHAPTER 9

The Shaman's Quest

We have seen how the heroes of the ancient Celts dealt with that empty stage in life wherein a man comes to the "dark and fearsome wood." We have followed some of them on the transcendent journey to the Land of Youth, a journey which recollects the astral experiences of Stone Age shamans. But what has all of this to do with us?

The fact of the matter is: the shamanistic journey itself is something of which we now stand in great need.

Western civilization has reached a dichotomous standstill, an emotional impasse. According to Jung, this crisis was prefigured, perhaps even prophetically apperceived, by the medieval authors of the Grail Legend. They were aware, whether consciously as practitioners of Hermetic lore or simply with the unconscious knowledge of creative artists, that the medieval West was beginning to lean towards an overdevelopment of the intellect that threatened to eclipse emotional wholeness altogether. Time has proved the Grail writers correct—the uncontrolled feelings and heady mindfulness of our culture have divided our souls.

Our European forebears once held to what we may call the Old Ways, ways founded upon a reverent acknowledgment of earth, wind, fire, water, and the invisible ethers permeating the atmosphere around us. The great deciduous forests of ancient Europe teemed with wildlife—the bison and aurochs, boar and deer, the bear and wolf and the wild hawk. Our ancestors, who shared the forest with its animal inhabitants, respected the enduring power of these other creatures. They knew that they themselves needed to embody the same empowerment in order to survive the harsh realities of life. Their earliest religion was shamanism; from this experiential core evolved the great mythologies of the Vikings, Greeks, and Celts.

Even after the advent of Christianity, the ordinary people— from whom most of us are, after all, descended—remembered a great deal of the Old Religion. They remembered the use of healing herbs, of animal powers, of the phases of the moon and the changes of the seasonal tides. Their feelings and emotions were courted by the weather and the patterns of the stars in the sky. They held tight to the wildness in the soul.

But when our ancestors arrived in the New World, they found a different land. The familiar old spirits of European woodlands—the gnomes, elves, and fairies—did not dwell in the Americas. Different spirits called from the lakes and waterfalls and forests of a different land. We might have learned to orient ourselves properly in the new magical environment had we paid heed to those who did know and understand the spirit of the land. But with the exception of a few voyageurs, mountain men, and other renegades, the European settlers seldom sat in council with Native Americans. Our own hold on the ancient ways was by that time a bit too tenuous or, in some cases, altogether absent. We had already surrendered to that loss of soul the Grail writers had predicted centuries earlier. We paid heed to Pilgrims and Puritans, the advocates of a more exclusive faith. Instead of learning the ways of the new land, we sought to destroy the people who could have taught us.

And so we continued to bind and limit our feeling natures—and our wildness—in new extremes of intellectual or spiritual rigidity, new extremes of isolation. And now it is part of our task—part of our shamanic quest—to reclaim it.

Do we still remember genuine spiritual ecstasy? Perhaps not. But surely we remember how it feels to be a teenager. Following the onset of puberty, the emotions flow in a torrent of unrestrained passion. The desire nature is obsessed with the body and its appearance—and with the appearance of other bodies as well. Girls want to be popular and fall in love; boys want to be with popular love-struck girls. And if acne or parental restrictions make sensual or sexual satiation next to impossible, there are drugs and alcohol to calm or further ignite teenage fantasies.

During that phase of life we ride on an emotional roller coaster. We are alive with feeling, our world filled with exquisite pleasure and, simultaneously, with exquisite pain. Someday we will grow up—which means, attain a balance. But during those years most of us are closer to the "psychic" or feeling realms than we will ever be again.

The esoterically minded cite physical reasons for this phenomenon. Hormones aside, there exists a long and narrow tube, similar to a drinking straw, connecting the cerebral cortex to the base of the spine. Thus this tube spans the entire length of the spinal cord, about which is bound the central nervous system. Throughout this area of the body we also find the endocrine system, including the thyroid, adrenal, and pituitary glands. These glands produce internal secretions that are carried by the blood or lymph to some part of the body whose functions they regulate or control. The seven subtle centers of power or chakras which feature strongly in Eastern meditative traditions are said to be imaged in the endocrine system. Prior to the onset of puberty, the spinal tube is open, allowing for an intercommunicative flow of energy among the various chakras. This is one reason why prepubescent children are so imaginative, creative, and expressive. They are still attuned with Nature, with the wild, free, instinctual, primal soul. Following puberty, however, the hollow in the tube closes down—hence the temporary insanity (sometimes approximating the wisdom of the sages) which we experience when we enter adolescence. Our inner circuits become blocked and consequently we spend our youth attempting to regain the feelings we have lost. But in most cases we must wait until we have reached the summit of our ascent of the worldly mountain—i.e., midlife—before we can accomplish this with genuine success.

The soul-searching of the midlife process is both painful and enlightening. We may stop in our tracks, realizing that a marriage no longer works or a particular career no longer suits us. We may realize that the time has come to trade in our conventional Oldsmobile for a motorcycle and head out on the open road to nowhere. The midlife period of transformation is a cathartic time. It generates a whole new world of self-discovery. It can be an accident waiting to happen or a lightning flash of inventive re-awakening. The choice belongs to us: to go with what is familiar, albeit subject to rules, regulations, and restrictions, or to enter the mode of the brave new world of the spirit.

At such a time a man may receive a call from his inner Warrior, as did King Cormac, to awaken from the dream (or nightmare!) of his life asleep. Sometimes the swan or stag will dash across the dreamer's vision, as it did for Cuchulain and Pwyll. Sometimes the wild old green guy himself will tap a man on the shoulder, as with Gawain, and make his hairy presence known. But it is most often the anima, the female soul or woman within, who calls a man back into wakefulness. Like Dante's Beatrice, she is the glowing inner figure who guides us through realms unknown. (After all, another name for the Land of Youth was the Castle of Damsels.)

The anima never screeches, like a harried fishwife, "Get off the couch and take out the garbage, you lazy S.O.B.!" Instead, she whispers sweetness in and around his ear (or lower) and makes him want to stand up and sing, or lie spent but in the proper frame of heart and mind.

The anima bestows upon a man everything which is contrary to his expectation. A man's typical expectation (at least in our society) is to get married, have children, and work from 9:00 to 5:00 in order to maintain the status quo for his family. His expectation is that he will have to surrender his dreams and live a "normal" life. The wife, the girlfriend, the mother-in-law, the sister, or the nosy next-door neighbor with the rollers in her hair may compel a man to do what is expected, but the anima impels a man to derive satisfaction from everything inventive, eccentric, surprising, unexpected.

The anima provides men with mystery and wonder, the childlike joy that fuels their creative passion and brings dreams through to fruition. She is a phantom cheerleader, madly waving her pompoms in your direction and daring you to make the final touchdown. She is the seductive sex slave, teasing you into impassioned submission by demanding your life-force as well as your love. Like Iseult the sorceress, she enthralls you with her magic spells, potions, and charms. She can make you believe you are the greatest magician in the land: wise Gandalf Greycloak or the Dark Lord Sauron. Whether good, bad, or ugly, you are her savior and her king. She, ever your devoted subject, is the sparkling jewel in your royal crown.

But all that glitters is not gold. So they say. Interesting to note, it is also the female soul that causes a man to neglect his primal self, his inner Wild Man. Even as the anima may awaken a man, so may she keep him in a death-like sleep of ignorance. Nimue locked Merlin in a cave or a tree for a thousand years. King Arthur lost Camelot over his love for Guinevere, and battled upon numerous occasions with the sorceress Morgan le Fay; both women brought Arthur to his knees but, fittingly enough, it was the sorceress who in time took him to Avalon, the Land of Promise. Pwyll slept in a cold and loveless bed next to Arawn's dark queen but in the end won for his wife bright Rhiannon, goddess of eternal life and queen of the Land of Youth.

Thus it would seem that a man must suffer at the hands of his own anima, must lie awake in the throes of an emotional darkness which has its origin in his "lady soul," before that soul deems him worthy of receiving a revelation, a vision, a glimpse of the truth and beauty inherent within him. She awakens him from the dark sleep of his isolation and leads him back to the Grail Castle, to that unity of all things which will heal his armored heart. And to do so, she casts him—typically in the middle of life—into a different kind of sleep, not of isolation but of rich and vivid dreams.

Psychologically, this sleep is in fact a period of gestation wherein the dreamer is carried—in the womb of that fluid consciousness occultists call the astral plane—all the way from spiritual conception to a rebirth of purpose in the outer world. At such times a man may seem distracted, lost in daydreams, dead to the world around him. But in fact he is developing a plan in the mind which will soon pierce the heart and galvanize his feelings once more. He is actualizing his future in the realm of the Otherworld.

When we are in such electrifying times, we partake of the wild mystical abandon of the shaman. But there is a vital difference. The shaman enters a state of transcendent awareness at will and for a specific reason. He climbs the World Tree to the land of the gods in order to seek a vision which will heal his people. When he is finished, he lays aside the ecstatic state of consciousness until he has need of it again. Were we able to call upon such a controlled state of ecstasy during our own crises, we would probably have a better sense of what to do. But a modern man is all too likely to slip into a trance wherein he merely dreams his life away, caught up in the dictates of society, the tube, and a six-pack of beer. How can he escape back into his "medicine man" self? What will induce a man to acquire knowledge, empowerment, or a simple desire to help others? How can a man who has slept for so long begin to see the light shining in the darkness?

One answer is that he may consciously return to what we have called the Old Ways, employing whatever blend of healing, magic, sorcery, or Wicca serves him as a balm for self-resolution, whatever serves to regain the shamanic state.

A shaman is capable of seeing a wonder, changing the weather, healing the sick, or conversing with the dead. Nevertheless, he is for the most part an ordinary man, though with an extraordinary sense of the sacred, the profane, and the ridiculous. He may be difficult to locate, but if one has need of him he will appear. He may appear (as he did to one of the authors) as an old man, nearly toothless, frying up liver in his cottage inside the great stone ring of Avebury, shouting above the sound of the TV. Or, in a more American context, he may come straight off the reservation, dressed in baseball cap, torn jeans, and an expensive pair of Reeboks. His

Shaman and Apprentices

magical paraphernalia—the eagle talons, smudge wands, crystals, herbs, and sacred tobacco—may well be kept in a briefcase rather than a deerskin pouch. And one is certainly more likely to be treated in the back bedroom of a city apartment rather than in a cave or tepee. But when a shaman opens his magic bag (or brief-case) and smudges you with sage or cleanses your aura with eagle feathers, you will have embarked upon the Otherworld journey just the same.

Your eyes may be closed, but your ears will be open. You may hear the sound of distant singing. Even if you don't actually hear it, you may feel this music as a rumble deep down in your belly. Waves of sound reverberate to fill your being, spreading upward from your innermost center to fill your heart, throat, feelings, and thoughts, flowing downward to stir your sexuality and your sense of certainty. The music is the shaman's light and guide through the abyss of the soul. Follow the sound and you will surely see the light, the color, the shapes and forms native to the Otherworld.

In order to journey through the Otherworld, a man must become proficient at seeing with his eyes closed, his senses alert and ready. The Otherworld has its own terrain. There are plants and creatures which are indigenous to it. There are helpful as well as harmful enti-ties with whom one must deal. It is easy to get lost in the Other-world. There are no maps, just feelings and intuition to see you through. Provided, that is, that you can find your way into the Oth-erworld in the first place. The entrance may be very, very small. In Native American and Polynesian traditions, there is often an aper-ture in the earth which leads down to the middle of the unknown, a fourth dimension in linear time. You might reach your destination through a deserted fox den, or a coyote hole littered with scat. Maybe an anthill beckons you to navigate its many winding pas-sageways. A mouse house will do, or a moss-covered tree bole. In Celtic tradition, a small gap opens in reality, and you ride through the mist into unknown worlds. Or you drift across the sea, across a lake, until a fair island beckons in the haze. However the Other-world appears to you, the question is: Can you make your mind small enough (or large enough) to fit inside? Can you make your thoughts, your worries, and the music on the radio station go away?

The shamanistic state of consciousness is similar to the part of ourselves which we contact in meditation—though a shaman's transcendent state is filled with imagery, color, and resonance rather than with absolute stillness or detachment. In order to assist the reader in linking up with the Otherworld voyager within himself, we have designed a group of exercises based on the four male archetypes: Warrior, Lover, Magician, and King. One need not be in a midlife crisis in order to begin the voyage! Let us remember that one of the problems men have in our society is that they have lost the ability to allow their spirits to take flight at any time or at any age.

Preparation for the Voyage
This preparatory exercise is intended to sharpen one's interior senses—a necessary prerequisite for regaining the shamanic state of consciousness. You will need the help of a friend as well as the following tools:

- A chair to sit in

- A flower

- A scarf (preferably white and made of silk)

- A candle

- A plate containing wheat bread, sea salt, and natural honey

- Some pre-recorded music of a "traditional" character (Celtic, of course, is fine)

Dim the lights in the room in which you are working. Place the above-mentioned tools on a table within easy reach. Sit upright in your chair, facing the east. Plant your feet firmly on the floor and let your hands rest in your lap. Close your eyes. Breathe slowly, deeply, and rhythmically. Inhale through your nose, feeling the breath fill your diaphragm and stomach. Hold each breath for as long as is comfortable, then slowly release it through your mouth. Continue until you feel completely relaxed.

When your body, mind, and emotions have been stilled, mentally surround yourself with an oval of brilliant white light, beginning at your feet and extending to the top of your head. Immerse yourself in the light. Let your breathing merge with the light until breath and light are one.

Nod your head or signal your friend in some other agreed-upon manner. Now he will turn on the music, which should be leveled to begin very softly, almost imperceptibly. Allow the sound to permeate your being. As the music begins to rise in volume, let your friend take up the flower and pass it slowly under your nose until he can see that you are breathing deeply of its essence.

Next, your friend will take up the silk scarf and begin to swirl it around you until you can consciously feel the breeze created by its movement. Eventually, the scarf should lightly brush against your skin. Experience this as pure sensation.

Next, your friend will take up the lighted candle and bring it close to you so that you can feel its heat on your face.

Finally, your friend will bring forward the plate of food. He will take up a small piece of wheat bread, dip it into the salt, and place it in your mouth. Receive the food with your total attention, placing your whole consciousness in the bread as you chew and swallow it. Repeat the same process, this time with the honey rather than the salt. Once again, put your total attention into the taste.

Now your friend lowers the music. You drift back into the oval of white light surrounding your body. Become conscious of your feet on the floor and open your eyes as the light fades away.

The Warrior
The Warrior has a tendency to jump into the shaman's foxhole, or ride into the Otherworldly mist, without even looking. Once inside the magical parameters, he may attempt to fight anything that comes his way. This sort of courage is admirable and sometimes even necessary, but it requires conscious control. Not all the phenomena encountered in the Otherworld are inimical to us; we must know when to accept as well as when to resist. The Warrior's fierce responses arise from his aloneness, his sense of armored isolation. The following exercise focuses on giving the Warrior the sense of unity with all Nature which is necessary if he is to navigate the Otherworld waters with love and acceptance as well as with courage.

Sit in a straight-backed chair, facing the east. If the weather permits, move your chair outside and perform this meditation in the open air.

Let your feet rest firmly on the ground and your hands loosely in your lap. Close your eyes; breathe deeply and regularly. Relax. Become one with the inflow and outflow of your breathing pattern.

Surround your body with a large oval of brilliant white light. Acknowledge the presence of the light. Feel the safety and empowerment within its protective sphere. Begin to mingle the light with the rhythm of your breathing, knowing that each inhalation feeds your inner body, your internal organs, your blood, with healing light, and that each exhalation filters out impurities from your bloodstream. Continue for several minutes.

Imagine that you are in an open meadow with the sun shining brightly overhead. A gentle breeze rustles through the grass and the heather, causing movement among the new spring wildflowers. Immerse yourself in the beauty that surrounds you. Feel the warmth of the sun and the wind caressing your body. It is a yellow, golden wind that swirls about your entire being. Allow the bright yellow breeze to light upon your head and face in a soft clockwise whirling motion. Hold on to the sensation for a few moments.

Now focus your attention on the wind moving through the grass and the flowers. Imagine it as a verdant green breeze, rising up from the earth and blowing toward you. Feel it reaching your body, whirling in counterclockwise motion from your throat to the top of your thighs. Meditate for several moments on its presence.

Feel the warmth of the bright golden sun overhead. Feel the cool green grass beneath your feet. Now imagine the yellow breeze whirling above your head and suddenly flowing down in a clockwise spiral, passing over, in, and through the green wind which circles counterclockwise about your torso, then continuing to swirl down from the top of your thighs to the soles of your feet. Experience this sensation for a few moments.

Finally, become aware of an invisible sun behind the worldly sun overhead. Imagine this internal sun as a bright white all-pervading orb infinitely greater than the physical sun. Sense its presence as the vast consciousness which embodies all wisdom, knowledge and understanding. Allow the yellow and green winds to be absorbed in this brilliant white sun until it alone remains.

Recognize this invisible sun as being one with the white oval of light which surrounds your body. Become conscious once more of the inflow and outflow of your breath. As you breathe in, feel the white light illuminating every cell of your body. Allow deep feelings of love and gratitude to well up within your heart. Offer up these feelings to the universe with each outward breath. Say to yourself: "I am one in unity with all life." Meditate on this image and thought for several minutes before returning to full waking consciousness.

The Lover
The Lover tries to charm his way into the Castle of Damsels, seduce the inhabitants, and return to physical reality emotionally satiated and psychically unscathed. Some of this type of behavior is necessary, but one needs to be careful when one is sleeping around in the psychic dark. The following exercise, in the form of a voyage to the Castle of Damsels, is slow and deliberate, for the Lover must learn to travel in the realm of the anima with respect and gentleness, rather than with pride and bravado.

Sit comfortably in a straight-backed chair, feet planted firmly on the floor and your hands held loosely in your lap. Have beside you a glass of water (or, if you are already deep into Celtic or pagan practices, use a real chalice). Drink the water. This is an action of symbolic purification.

Now close your eyes and become aware of your breathing. Bring the air deeply into your body through the nose and slowly release it through the mouth. Continue to breathe in this manner until you feel your entire body relax into the continuous rhythm of the universe.

Mentally create an oval of white light around your entire body, beginning at your head and ending at your feet. Silently acknowledge the presence of the light. Know that you are secure within the safety and protection of its radiant sphere.

Now imagine a vibrant lake of royal blue light stretched out before you. The center of your being is upon the shoreline, which is thick with reeds and humming with the sound of birds. Over the lake, a crescent-shaped barge approaches through the mist. In the barge stand three women, robed in black. Perhaps they are beautiful; perhaps their features are insubstantial, indistinct. Enter the barge.

Now you begin to drift away from the shore, into the mist-haunted blue of the lake. Immerse yourself in the liberating sensation of timelessness. Allow all thought and emotion to melt away as you sail further into the blue cosmos.

Now imagine that you see before you, far in the distance, a tiny spot of radiant silver light. Watch as the light grows larger and brighter. Feel your barge being drawn into this light, which has now become a glowing silver line stretched out upon the horizon. Notice that you are being pulled toward this silvery horizon by a silken cord, also of silver, which is connected to your heart. Allow the cord to pull you and your barge effortlessly along until you are enveloped in the silver light. Within this shining aura all negative habit patterns are burned away. Feel yourself released from the past, renewed, and regenerated so that you may start life afresh. Meditate on this feeling for several moments.

Finally, direct your inner vision homeward, your thoughts focused upon the reedy shore from which you embarked. Picture your entire being once again flooded with vibrant blue as your barge emerges from the infinity of silver light. Almost immediately, you and your vessel are back on the shore. Step out of the craft and bid farewell to the women in the barge as they slowly sail away back into the mist.

Now imagine that you can see your own reflection in the waters of the lake. Become one with the silent waters. Say to yourself:

"I am one with the waters of the Land of Youth. I am one with the Great Mother Deep. All creatures and things are but reflections of the One. I recognize that I do nothing of myself, but continue my journey for the sake of that power which has sent me forth."

Return your attention to your breathing. Make a silent sensory offering of love and gratitude to the white light that has protected you, and slowly return to full waking consciousness.

The Magician

The Magician will be in his element when he enters the Otherworld. After all, he is the one who knows all the tricks; his intuition is well honed, his intellect sharp and aware. But, as the Hermetic books affirm: "That which is above is like that which is below." The Magician had best be certain that his mental house is truly in order before attempting the trip into the depths of the unknown.

Like the Warrior, the Magician may be something of an isolationist, overly proud of his intellect and his skill. The following exercise focuses on the Magician's heart rather than his mind, for it is with a clear and hopeful heart that he must make his entry into the Otherworldly realms.

Sit comfortably in a chair, facing east, feet planted firmly on the floor. Rest your hands softly in your lap. Close your eyes. Pay attention to the inflow and outflow of your breathing. Breathe in deeply through your nose, letting the air fill your abdomen, then breathing out again slowly through the mouth. Continue until you are physically, mentally, and emotionally relaxed and you feel at one with the rhythm of the universe around you.

Imagine an oval of brilliant white light surrounding your body. Acknowledge the presence of the light; know that you are protected and safe within its radiant sphere.

Now, in your mind's eye, form a ball of vibrant red light hovering in front of you, to the east, at the level of your abdomen.

Then imagine another ball of light, this one bright orange, just above the glowing red sphere.

Finally, imagine a ball of clear violet light and mentally place it above the orange sphere. You should now have three luminous balls of light, beginning with violet at the top, then orange, then red. The orange sphere should be centered at the level of your heart.

Now image the three balls of glowing light traveling around you in a clockwise motion. Note how they move from east to south to west to north, leaving streams of light which surround you like three glowing rings. Let the circle spin faster, becoming a single pulsating ring of violet, orange, and red flame. Draw this circle of living light inward, and slowly allow it to be absorbed into your heart.

Picture the circle now as a glowing red flame, tipped with orange and violet, at rest within your heart. Feel the warmth of the flame ignite your senses with unconditional love for all creatures and things. Reflect upon this sensation for several minutes. Then return your attention to the original oval of white light which is still surrounding you. Offer up thoughts and feelings of love and gratitude to the light.

As you slowly return to full waking consciousness, remember that divine love and protection are with you always.

The King

The King is confident; he seldom journeys alone. He will bring many of his subjects with him—mentally, at least—and therefore be well protected from harm. Or he may travel in disguise, as Kings often do. In any event, he is the King, and anyone or anything encountered in the Otherworld will listen, obey, and succumb to his powerful skills. This is helpful too, but the King may actually need his back-up to get through.

Because it is the King's special task to unite with the spiritual energy of the land for which he serves as caretaker, this exercise makes use of the World Tree, the mystical center of the world. By becoming one with the World Tree, the King becomes one with the power of the land, with the earth itself.

This exercise should preferably be performed outdoors, using a real tree. If weather forbids, you may construct a tree in your imagination, and you may wish to imagine it as a true Celtic World Tree—a gigantic hazel stretching far and away into the infinite, its branches thick with nuts, a silver pool of water at its base.

Sit cross-legged on the ground, your back upright against the trunk of the tree, facing east. Take note of the rhythm of your breathing. Slow it down gradually as you breathe in deeply through your nose and release slowly through your mouth. Surround the tree—and yourself—with brilliant, shining white light. See the light glistening in the leaves of the World Tree like countless stars. Imagine the light shimmering down the trunk, which is now glowing in shades of muted copper-brown.

Focus your whole attention on the point where you contact the earth itself. Allow the natural electrical energy of the earth to rise slowly in your body, igniting at the base of the spine and spiraling in clockwise motion up to your waist in radiant swirls of blue-violet. Continue to draw the energy of the earth up your spinal column, flooding your body with more spirals of light—yellow this time—from your waist to your shoulders. Finally, envision whirling spirals of vibrant green light flowing up from your shoulders to the top of your head. Meditate on the colors and the sensations they induce for several minutes.

Then turn your attention to your breathing and to the tree. Imagine that the tree, just like your body, is vibrating in concentric circles of blue-violet, yellow, and green, moving upward from its base to the top of its leafy branches. Feel the life pulsing inside the tree and imagine that it too is breathing along with you. Recognize that you are one with this energy which you have drawn from deep inside the earth. Meditate on the earth as a living thing.

Begin to release the images very slowly. Finally, nothing remains but the earth, the tree, and you, still surrounded with white light. Offer up love and gratitude to the light for protecting you, to the tree for granting you shelter and companionship, and to the earth for giving you sustenance. Then return to ordinary waking consciousness.

CHAPTER 10

The Gods of Earth and Sea

We have followed a number of old Celtic heroes on their journeys to that pagan Grail Castle, the Land of Youth. We have brought them over the sea and through the mist. But what do they find and whom do they meet when they arrive there?

We may remember that the great warrior Cuchulain fell into a trance after attempting to shoot down an Otherworldly swan. While he lay enchanted, his faithful charioteer journeyed to the Otherworld to seek the reason for his master's peculiar sleep (Cuchulain himself makes the journey later in the story). The charioteer crossed a misty plain and sailed to an isle in the midst of a magical lake. There he reached the Otherworld, a great house ruled by two kings and guarded by a hundred and fifty warriors. Fifty of these warriors slept on beds placed at the right side of the Otherworldly hall, and fifty on beds placed at the left. The story continues:

The beds have round columns,
Beautiful posts, adorned with gold.

They gleam brightly in the light
Which comes from a stone, precious and brilliant.

At the door toward the west
On the side toward the setting sun,
There is a troop of grey horses with dappled manes,
And another troop of horses, purple-brown.

At the door toward the east
Are three trees of purple glass.
From their tops a flock of birds sing a sweetly drawn-out song
For the children who live in the royal stronghold.
There is a cauldron of invigorating mead,
For the use of the inmates of the house.
It never grows less; it is a custom
That it should be full forever.

There is a woman in the noble palace.
There is no woman like her in Erin.
When she goes forth you see her fair hair.
She is beautiful and endowed with many gifts.

Her words, when she speaks to anyone,
Have a marvellous charm.
She wounds every man to the heart
With the love she inspires.[1]

We may recognize the "precious and brilliant" stone as the same world axis Bran the Voyager encountered on his travels through the Land of Youth. We may recognize the trees of singing birds as images of that marvelous World Tree where Rhiannon's birds sing to us of poetry and magic.

But we are clearly in the realm of the medieval Grail Castle as well. The great house is none other than the castle itself, though Cuchulain's charioteer met two kings there rather than one. Even more filled with resonance, for our purposes, is the image of the beautiful woman who serves us mead from a magic cauldron.

Here, then, is the pagan original of the ghostly maiden whom Perceval saw walking through the Fisher King's hall carrying the Grail. And we may guess that the lady of the Grail Castle was originally Rhiannon herself, the queen of the Otherworld.

But who is the Fisher King?

Let us return to the tale of King Cormac, whom we left lost in a mist as he pursued a "calm gray-haired warrior." Upon emerging from the fog, he:

> *saw another royal stronghold, and another wall of bronze around it. There were four palaces therein. He entered the fortress and saw the vast palace with its beams of bronze, its wattling of silver, and its thatch of the wings of white birds.*[2]

Having discovered the Grail Castle, Cormac met a royal couple—the gray-haired warrior upon a throne, and a beautiful woman. He was feasted from the cauldron of plenty; his missing family was returned to him and he was given a marvelous cup. The lord of the Otherworld revealed himself as Manannan mac Lir, king of the Land of Promise.

Another Otherworld journey, one we have not yet examined, is that of Conn of the Hundred Battles, recorded in a tale entitled "The Phantom's Frenzy." Like Cormac, Conn reaches the Otherworld by riding across a Plain of Mist. He comes to a golden tree, and a house thirty feet long with a ridgepole of white gold. He and his companions enter the house and behold a girl, seated in a chair of crystal and wearing a crown of gold. Beside her is a vessel of gold and before her a golden cup. On the Otherworld throne is a phantom, who this time identifies himself as Lug. The woman is the Sovereignty of Ireland, whom we may remember from the story of Niall of the Nine Hostages (Chapter 5) as the indwelling feminine spirit of the land. She serves Conn and his companions ale and food.

The remarkable parallels between these ancient Irish tales and the medieval Grail legends should leave us with no doubts as to the identity of the Fisher King and the maiden of the Grail: they are the king and queen of the old Celtic Otherworld.

Though Conn the Hundred Fighter encountered an Other-world King who called himself Lug (the old Celtic deity Lugh), the Irish tales more often tell us that the ruler of the Land of Youth is Manannan mac Lir. The calm, gray-haired warrior who led Cormac through the mist proved to be none other than Manannan, and in the tale of Bran's great sea voyage, the travelers see Manannan mac Lir riding towards them over the waves in his chariot just as they approach Tir-na-nog.

As we have noted previously, the Irish Manannan—a deity so popular that his appearances were commonly reported up until the eighteenth century—is but another name for Manawyddan, son of Llyr, the magical hero of the *Mabinogion* who weds Rhiannon and rescues her from the clutches of the dark lord. Is the Grail King, therefore, simply a medieval recension of old Manawyddan?

Not quite. Robert de Boron, in one of the earliest versions of the Grail myth, names the king "Brons." Malory, writing in the 1400s, calls him "Pelles." An old Welsh folktale included in the *Mabinogion* names the Grail knight Peredur rather than Perceval.

It may seem, then, as if we have entered a realm of confusion and contradiction. Different names abound for the same characters. How can we make anything of all this?

In fact, there is a remarkable coherence underlying the apparent chaos. Some Celtic scholars have argued that all these names can be found in the first four "branches" of the *Mabinogion* in slightly different form: the name Brons, for instance, is derived from Bran, while Pelles derives from Pwyll and Peredur from Pryderi.[3]

And all of these individuals—including Manawyddan, the most common name for the Otherworldly king—seem originally to have been members of a tribe of deities called the Children of Llyr.

Our Indo-European ancestors typically recognized two distinct "families" or categories of gods—those who ruled over the starry heavens and those who ruled the earth and sea. The Greek Olympians, sky gods all, battled with and overthrew the more earthy, primordial Titans. The Norse Aesir, who included Odin and Thor among their numbers, kept up a constant state of dynamic tension with the earth and sea gods called the Vanir, who included more

Manannan mac Lir

sexual deities such as Freyr and Freyja and primal forces of Nature such as the sea god Njord.

In Celtic myth, the Tuatha de Danaan arrive in Ireland like resplendent sky gods and battle with the darker, hairier Fomorians. The term "Tuatha de Danaan" means "Children of Danu." These Children of Danu are equivalent to another celestial family called the Children of Don that figures powerfully in the Welsh *Mabinogion*. Gwydion of the Magic Harp, Math the Ancient, silvery Arianrhod and Lleu of the Skillful Hand may be numbered among these Children of Don.

But there is another family of gods in the *Mabinogion*, and this is the Children of Llyr. Though Llyr (an apparent sea god) never actually appears in the stories, his sons Bran and Manawyddan and his daughter Branwen certainly do. Manawyddan married Rhiannon, whose former husband was Pwyll; Pryderi was the son of Pwyll and Rhiannon. In the *Mabinogion's* Fourth Branch, Gwydion, the great magician of the Children of Don, steals the magic swine (animals sacred to the Underworld lord throughout Celtic myth) of Pryderi, initiating a battle in which Pryderi is killed. Here, then, we see yet another echo of the eternal war between the gods of the sky and the gods of earth and sea.

We shall be on the right track if we assume that the Grail King embodies the earth and sea energy of the Children of Llyr. But why does he seem, at one time or another, to bear all their names?

The answer, perhaps, is most clearly seen in the *Parzival* of Wolfram von Eschenbach. At the end of the story, after years of seeking to return to the Grail Castle, Parzival makes his second visit to that Otherworldly spot. Here he learns that he himself is to become the new Grail King! Why? Because he is, unbeknownst to himself till now, a member of the Grail family. All this time, he has been unwittingly searching for his own roots.[4]

Pwyll was succeeded by his son Pryderi; Llyr was presumably succeeded by Bran. This endless round of fathers and sons points to an essential psychological truth: every man must take the path of his fathers before him and awaken that earth-and-sea energy which is inherent within him, which is his primal essence as it was the essence of his fathers. For if the lordly Tuatha de Danaan represent the "sky" of our consciousness—our intellect, our aspiration, and our inherent godhood—then the Children of Llyr represent everything instinctual, unspoken, silent, and deep. A man's soul may rage like the sea, but it rages in silence, in the deep caverns below the waters. A man may travel below the earth and do battle there, like Pwyll against Havgan, to win the Goddess and thus give birth to springtime in his soul, but this battle is one which takes place deep below the surface of things.

A woman may look to the depths of her soul and discover a core of initiative, courage, energy, and passion, a dynamic, assertive, fiery self. However, a man may find (much to his surprise) what the alchemists called "a certain soft, prolific Venus" that seeks expression through the feeling nature. Love, affection, artistry, harmony, beauty, values, attraction, relating, and peace— all of these words describe the earth-and-sea power in a man's soul, that which remains hidden in plain sight.

Men and women are equal in spirit and intelligence. They are worlds apart in terms of physical and emotional orientation. When a man loses himself to find his soul, he often awakens an irresistible force; the instinctual promptings of his own innate sensitivity, spirituality, music, imagination, idealism, and dreams, manifesting as sudden change, rebellion, independence, originality, eccentricity, and liberation of the senses. So it is that within the soul of a man we find the mysterious impressionism of the feminine self, which is to say, the subjective, passive, emotional self.

The sea represents the nature of movement in water, the electromagnetic vibration which animates all things. It is a transitional and mediating agent comprised of ether, air, and earth. The sea is the source of both life and death. We are born within the ocean of the womb, and we return to the mother, to earth, to die.

A man returns to the feminine in order to leave his old self behind. But this does not mean that he *becomes* feminine! This has been a premier case of mistaken male identity which has taken its toll among men in our society, whether they are gay, straight, crazy, or some combination of all three. A "real" man is a man who is in touch with the essence of his spirit. He follows the dictates of his heart into regions unknown. He journeys to the center of the earth and learns the limits, capabilities, and potentialities of his physical body. He explores the uncharted depths of the sea and receives wisdom and understanding of his secrets, his sanctuaries, his self-undoings, and his strengths. He is not blind-sided and broken by the shrill cry of neo-fascist feminists who proclaim that a man need be gelded, weeping, and compliant to the whims of his female partner if he is to qualify as the perfect New Age bedmate. A "real" woman would fight to constrain the urge to spit on the whining, sniveling, "soft" male who has swallowed the fly in the feminist ointment hook, line, and sinker.

Better a man return to his own kingly domain, the warrior's lust for blood and battle. Rather he should slip his lover's heart through a crack in the back door than wear it red and bleeding down the sleeve of his starched white shirt. The magical man, the *sha*man, fights the overt injustice plaguing the world, as well as dragons, demons, and unseen foes. He now needs to fight for the right to be himself, in body, mind, heart, and soul. To do this, one must learn tough self-love, a process wherein one casts oneself into the wilderness, the dark forest, fen and fern, the dry and solitary desert, the salted mist of offshore lands, the breathless space of mountains. All of these places reek of desolation yet teem with the wild, primal freedom of life lived without fear.

D.H. Lawrence said it well in his 1928 essay, "New Mexico":

> *In the oldest religion, everything was alive, not supernaturally but naturally alive. There were only deeper and deeper streams of life, vibrations of life more and more vast.... The whole life effort (of mankind) was to get his life into contact with the elemental life of the cosmos...*

All is alive in Nature and we are a part of the wonder of all creation. The time has come for us to rediscover the wonder within ourselves.

It is this primal wonder, this depth charge in the soul which we find symbolized by the Children of Llyr, the gods of earth and sea—and it is here that we encounter the archetype which is perhaps the best known in the emerging men's movement: the Wild Man.

We have all come to know (and hopefully to love) the Wild Man within. When civilized man is confronted with conflicts at home or on the job, he tries to reason with the situation. Wild Man, the king of unreason, may either punch out his antagonist or just walk away laughing. When civilized man is nagged by his wife and kids, he backs down and gives in, for he is a *good* man. Wild Man drives away in his pickup truck for a solo camping venture, leaving them all to whine and fuss at each other. If civilized man has a "mother problem," he talks about it with his therapist. Wild Man dances on the old biddy's grave. Wild Man sings in the shower, sleeps out in the woods, stops to smell the wildflowers. Civilized man loves a well-groomed yard in a well-groomed community; Wild Man loves vastness, openness, the splendid disorder of Nature.

In Celtic mythology, the Wild Man is typified by the god Cernunnos, Lord of the Animals. He wears antlers on his head and a snake around his waist. On the Gundestrup Cauldron, he is shown in full lotus posture, surrounded by animals. Though his traces are archaeologically elusive and mythically almost invisible, some believe he is the oldest god of all, and that the shaman with antlers carved on the walls of a Paleolithic cave site in France is his close kin.[5] Modern-day pagans revere him as the god whose devotees died in the witch trials; the magister of the Sabbat, who danced wearing the antlers or horns of a stag or goat, they say, was old Cernunnos.

In Paleolithic times, a man would dress in the skins of the animal he wished to kill in the hunt. Many times this animal was a deer or stag. He would pray for the creature to cross his path, so that his woman might have a skin to cover her and so that his children might be fed. He would pray to the animal and ask for its flesh with a promise that death would be swift and merciful.

When a shaman required powerful medicine to protect the tribe or heal the sick, he would don the skin and antlers of a stag and pray for help. This animal was chosen because it represents compassion, courage, and gentleness in the face of adversity and evil. Inherent in the nature of the stag is the ability to love both light and dark and to create safety, peace, and security. Thus it is sacred, akin to the divine.

So the antlered one, the horned one, came to be revered as a god, though in reality he was symbolic of a *man*, exercising his potential for goodness. His respect for and devotion to Nature and her laws provided him with the perfect consort, Nature herself. Fire, water, earth, and sky; insect, fish, and fowl; the warm-bodied, four-legged creatures of the wood—these were the fruit of his loins, his children. So he taught his sons to hunt and pray and protect and nourish and heal that which was all around them. And he protected, loved, and cherished his grandmothers, mothers, sisters, wives, and daughters. Cernunnos did not dance alone, but danced the dance of life holding tight the hand of Nature—the outstretched, yielding palm of the goddess who is woman.

Cernunnos was the Lord of the Forest. One of the few mythological references to him is found in the tale entitled "Owain" in the *Mabinogion*. He is portrayed as a dark giant of a fellow who has only to call in order to be surrounded by hundreds of wild things.[6] He may even have been the original of Robin Hood—hero, trickster, lover, and Wild Man—for the "Robin Hood dances" performed on May Day in the Elizabethan era featured a Robin Hood who wore antlers on his head! But for our purposes, it is most important than Cernunnos was the Lord of the Otherworld. A relief sculpture from Gallo-Roman France shows him seated on the Underworld throne, like Hades or Pluto, wrapped in his snake and crowned with antlers. His name is even carved above his head. And there is a cornucopia, a horn of plenty, at his feet.[7] Is it, perhaps, yet another metaphor for the Grail?

If Cernunnos ruled in the Otherworld, he may have been the pagan original of the Grail King. Let us note that on the Gundestrup Cauldron, as Cernunnos sits with his serpent in hand and surrounded by wild animals, he is sitting next to a great vessel, reminiscent of the Cauldron of Rebirth which figures in Bran's tale. Is he guarding it?

He may at one time have had to *win* it—just as each new participant in the quest, each child of wild old Llyr, must win the Grail for himself, again and again. An Irish tale tells of one Conall Cearnach, a warrior of Ulster and companion of Cuchulain. Conall sets out to win a treasure which is guarded by a great serpent. But the

Cernunnos in the Grail Castle Mandala

serpent, instead of battling the hero, entwines itself around Conall's waist, becoming a part of him.

This may seem to be just one of many dragon-slaying legends, and not a very convincing reference to the serpent of Cernunnos, save for one minor detail—the word "Cearnach." In the name Cernunnos, the first syllable, *cern*, means "horn"—hence his title the Horned One. The *cearn* in Cearnach may also mean "horn," and thus Conall too may well be the Horned One, winning the "treasure hard to attain" which is equivalent to the Grail.[8]

The Grail King, as we have seen, is none other than the king of the old Celtic Otherworld. Symbolic of the primal, Wild Man energies of earth and sea, he has had many names: Pwyll, Bran, Pryderi, and Manawyddan. His earliest name, and his most primal form, may well have been Cernunnos, the antlered one.

But there is one all-important difference between the Otherworld Lord of ancient Celtic myth and the Fisher King of later centuries: the Fisher King is gravely *wounded.*

The present-day Cernunnos is a very lonely god-man. His skins drag in the dirt and his antlers droop—or else are stunted or broken altogether. Sometimes he has no antlers at all. He has been exiled from his consort, the goddess woman. A man comes into this world to a short time of awareness between birth and death, and he is, as are all creatures, entitled to the comfort of a mate.

Nature in the 1990s has proven herself to be a tempestuous partner at best. Hurricanes, floods, earthquakes, and strange weather patterns; AIDS, cancer, and hantaviruses—none of these pestilences currently assailing the creatures and things of our planet make Nature an enticing bedmate. In fact, she has lifted her veil to reveal one angry mother! And her female worshippers seem to have followed suit. Today's goddess cults, justifiably enraged with what may be considered a mass repudiation of Nature, have in turn expelled men (the ostensible culprits) from the society of women. Man, *sha*man, once venerated for his ability to transmit the powers of sun and moon, light and dark, to his people, no longer has a kingdom, a home, a family, a tribe, with whom to share his medicine.

How did Cernunnos come to be such a bad guy? There are several answers to that question.

Perhaps the greatest display of shadow-shift in man's consciousness occurred when patriarchy came to seem like a better solution than matriarchy to the eternal problem of the relationships between men and women. Patriarchy, born in the Bronze Age, in time careened toward the dangerous conclusion that there is only one god (in this case, a Father). What the patriarchs failed to realize (or perhaps knew all too well but simply chose to ignore) was the fact that earlier polytheistic pagan societies—including the matriarchies of the Aegean and the Near East—likewise believed there was only one deity or universal consciousness, whose divine essence was simply expressed through many semblances and forms.

Some of these semblances and forms were supremely discomforting to the patriarchs of yore. Poet-scholar Robert Graves cites an example from ancient Palestine, wherein the Jews forbade the further participation of priestesses in all sacred rites. It was thought that women had an unsettling effect on religious life: they introduced an element of sexuality which would surely lead honest, god-fearing men to confuse eroticism with mystical ecstasy (although for many pagans, there was little or no difference between the two). It was believed that the promiscuous pagan displays which characterized festival times would loosen family ties and wreak chaos in the social system—as if the Great Goddess were responsible for seducing men to their folly.[9]

The early fathers of the Christian church followed suit. As late as the fourth century AD, the Gnostics still proclaimed that Mary Magdalene was the consort of Jesus, his partner in the sacred dance. This dangerous notion was eradicated shortly thereafter.

Jung once wrote that three is the patriarchal number, exemplified in the Christian trinity. Originally that trinity was comprised of the Father, the Son, and a vital spirit symbolized by the dove (bird of the goddess Venus), and who may have once represented either a divine androgyne or a feminine wisdom principle called Sophia. In time, however, that vital wisdom spirit became a mysterious Holy Ghost, of no identifiable gender whatsoever, leading to the implication that all aspects of God were masculine in nature.

When Christianity reached Celtic lands, the missionaries discovered that the "natives" had their own trinity—or, rather, two trinities. The Indo-European peoples, like the Christians from warmer Mediterranean lands, regarded three as a most important number. There were three levels of society—the rulers or kings (including priests), warriors, and tradespeople. Each of these classes of society had its deity or group of deities. Lugh or Lleu, for example, was primarily a god of Druids and kings; Nuada of the Silver Hand was the warrior of the Tuatha de Danaan; earthy divinities like the Dagda and healers like the Irish physician Diancecht were sacred to tradespeople.

The other "trinity" was feminine in nature, and had been known all over Europe long before the Indo-Europeans made their appearance there (which suggests that Jung may have been wrong in regarding three as a purely masculine number). This older trinity was comprised of the three aspects of the Great Goddess. She was the Sky, Earth, and Underworld. She was the moon, new, full and waning, as well as the three stages of life symbolized by the lunar cycle: nymph or maiden, mother, and crone. She was spring, summer, and winter; birth, procreation, and death. As the moon, she was the bringer of light to dark places. She had a star son who was both her lover and, eventually, her sacrificial victim; he too was a creature of light and darkness, alternately lover and serpent.

These Celtic trinities had a psychological advantage over the later Christian version: they were in harmony with the natural currents of life and the seasons. The more rigid Christian concept led to a suppression of the flow of our emotions, feelings, and responses. And because most of us of European descent still struggle with the patriarchal mindset of the early Christians, we labor to reclaim our flexibility, to dance in harmony with the tides of change.

We have noted earlier that Cernunnos is often depicted holding a ram-headed serpent in his hands. Does this suggest that he is the Great Mother's lover-son who manifests at times as the serpent? Let us note also that early Iron Age art shows Cernunnos wearing a silver torque or open neck-ring, sometimes around his neck, sometimes held in his hands. This has often been interpreted as a feminine or lunar symbol, thus suggesting once again that Cernunnos is indeed the lover, the son, the Goddess' partner in the sacred dance.[10]

Some scholars have believed that the symbolism of Cernunnos implies that the Celts attached greater importance to the god than the goddess.[11] (Pagan feminists would, of course, violently disagree.) Granted, it was primarily the Celtic man who risked life and limb to get meat and feed the tribe. However, Celtic women sometimes hunted alongside the men; they often carried swords into battle as well. They were revered for ripening a man's seed in the dark, soft hollow of their bodies. It was not until the advent of Christianity that Celtic women were denied their rightful, equable places of honor among the people.

Spirit (the Goddess as Sky) in the form of intuition is reflected through the unconscious (the Underworld Goddess) into self-conscious awareness (the Earth, whether Father or Mother). The feminine principle is neither above man nor below him. It is, however, a magic mirror, receiving images as the moon receives the light of the sun. When a man looks into the mirror of life, sees only his own image, and neglects to remember the true nature of lunar "reflection" (meditation, rumination, deliberation, cogitation, study, and thought), he produces a distorted self-image which is narcissistic in nature. When there is no Diana to dance with Cernunnos in the heart of the forest, there is no breath of life to fill the empty places in a man's soul.

Historically speaking, the mirror became distorted. Ancient cults were repressed by force during what feminist historians call the Burning Times—though men as well as women went to the stake. Some pagan customs, such as ritual dancing, sacred feasts, sexual license, and the worship of living forces with magical rites, were too deeply rooted to be removed from the European unconscious altogether. They were, however, reformulated to seem more Christian in character. Cernunnos was a casualty of such "reformulation."

In the beginning, Lucifer or Satan was a Near Eastern divinity linked with Venus as the Morning Star. How did he come to wear horns and hooves? Cernunnos, of course, as a stag, wore horns (or antlers) and had hooves. Nor was he the only horned and hooved divinity of pre-Christian Europe. Pan, Earth Father and Wild Man, with music in his soul and phallus erect, was another such deity, dancing through the forests of the European unconscious. These

Wild Men were the gods the Christians feared most, for they represented the flow of Nature and sexuality at its strongest and most powerful. Thus the devil, Lucifer himself, was given their attributes to make sure that everyone got the point.

By such historic paths were the God and Goddess robbed of their power—the Goddess surgically removed, the God twisted into a devil. The Wild Man became evil, the power of Nature itself equated with darkness and fear rather than with joy.

But there is another aspect to the Grail King's wound, one which is primarily spiritual, psychological, and mythic rather than historical. It is this mythic dimension of the sacred wound which is most likely to touch us personally—though our own personal histories cannot be entirely separated from the history of the race.

If we are to heal the wound in our own Cernunnos, as well as aid in the healing of his wild spirit in all men, we must understand in some depth the nature of the Grail King's wound.

Notes

1. Cross and Slover, *Ancient Irish Tales*, 188–9.

2. Ibid., 504–5.

3. Squire, *Celtic Myth and Legend*, 354–70.

4. Wolfram von Eschenbach, *Parzival* (citation to come).

5. Margaret A. Murray, *God of the Witches* (London: Oxford University Press, 1970), 23–4.

6. Gantz, *Mabinogion*, 192–216.

7. MacCana, *Celtic Mythology*, 44–8.

8. Ibid., 47.

9. Robert Graves, *King Jesus* (New York: Farrar Straus Giroux, 1984), 6.

10. T.C. Lethbridge, *Witches* (New York: Citadel Press, 1968), 34.

11. Ibid.

CHAPTER 11

The Sacred Wound

In myths the world over, we find the motif of the sacred wound which strikes a man in the thigh or the heel. The Greek smith-god Hephaestus suffered from a lame leg, and Achilles had his weakness in his famous heel. The Biblical patriarch Jacob was dragged out of his mother's womb by the heel, and later set his thigh "out of joint" while wrestling with an angel. The wise centaur Chiron also suffered such a magic wound, though different versions of the story place this wound in both heel and thigh. The Grail King, as we have seen, is also wounded in his thigh.

This magic wound is a quintessentially male archetype; there is no precise equivalent for the sacred wound in female mythologies. Of course it is true that everyone who is not whole is somehow wounded. As with a man, a woman's process begins when she experiences *separation* from the unity and completeness which is the source of all life and which is symbolized in myth by the archetype of the Great Mother. Hers remains an *invisible* wound which is not always apparent to the outside observer, in contrast to the male wound, which by virtue of its association with the heel or thigh is manifestly *visible*, at least in mythological terms. A woman's wound is cyclic in nature: at times she may be raised to heights of great joy, and at other times plummet down to the nether depths of despair. Rhiannon suffers such a wound of separation upon losing her only son Pryderi to the Otherworld. Later, as the *Mabinogion* tells us, she regains her son but in turn loses herself—she is taken to the Otherworld to dwell with the faery king under the mountain. But Rhiannon returns from the mountain's half-light into the sunlight of the real world, rescued by Pryderi and by her second husband, the magician Manawyddan. Thus we may say that a woman's wound is opened and closed via a psychological process of descent, death, and rebirth or resurrection. This is why most women tend to strive for fulfillment and completion on *interior* levels.

Separation is a necessary phase in a woman's process of death and rebirth. But for men, separation or isolation is simply the hero's natural state. Men strive not for interior completion, but for outer perfection. Though they may journey to the Otherworld for various reasons, they are not abducted into that realm after the manner of Rhiannon or the Greek Persephone. Their process is necessarily different from a woman's.

Many psychologists have seen the male "sacred wound" as sexual because of its connection with the thigh.[1] One version of the Grail Legend actually says that when the Grail King was wounded with a lance in the thigh, the poison from the metal seeped into his genitals. It is worth noting, also, that the land round about the Grail Castle has become a wasteland. It is barren; it cannot bear fruit. This, too, has been seen by some interpreters as a sexual symbol.[2]

The tale of Bran—whom, as we have seen, is one of the mythological gods upon whom the figure of the Grail King is ultimately based—is told in the Second Branch of the *Mabinogion*.[3] Bran, King of Wales, is the son of Llyr, god of the sea. He leads his knights to Ireland to rescue his sister Branwen from a cruel husband. In the course of the battle which ensues, the magic Cauldron of Rebirth which Bran gave to the King of Ireland as a wedding gift is destroyed. Thus we are obviously moving in the same world as the Grail Legend, for here we see the Grail itself and its loss. In this battle, Bran is wounded in the heel with a spear. On medical grounds alone, such a wound would not appear fatal. But this is a magic wound—the only cure is for Bran's remaining knights to put him to death! So they cut off his head. But that is not the end of it. His severed head begins to speak prophecy and is buried under a hill near what is now London to serve as a prophetic voice for a future yet unknown. The Welsh folktale version of the Grail Myth, also preserved in the *Mabinogion* and entitled "Peredur," tells us that a human head lay upon the silver serving dish in the Grail Castle.[4] Is this the head of Bran himself?

Bran's name means "crow" or "raven"—his sister Branwen is the "white raven." If we turn to ancient Greece, we may discover yet another crow or raven. Most scholars have assumed that the name of the god Cronus (better known to us under his Roman name of Saturn) is related to *chronos*, meaning time. In fact, our New Year's image of Father Time—hourglass, sickle, and long white beard —is comprised of the mythological attributes of Saturn. But poet-scholar Robert Graves links this name not only with *chronos* but with *coronis*, meaning crow or raven, and concludes that Bran is the Celtic equivalent of Cronus or Saturn.[5] That Saturn was associated with the raven in medieval times is clear, for the alchemists identify the melancholy *nigredo* or "blackening," the initial stage of their spiritual process, with Saturn as well as with the raven.

The Grail Legend itself supports this link between alchemy, Saturn, and the raven. As we have noted, the most overtly esoteric version of the Grail myth is the one authored by a medieval German knight named Wolfram von Eschenbach. Wolfram tells us that the suffering of the Grail King becomes unbearable when the moon is new and when Saturn is either rising or when it completes its orbital revolution.[6]

This unexpected connection between Bran's wound, the Fisher King's wound, and the planet Saturn requires some explanation. Saturn, as an astrological symbol, represents boundaries and limitations. The most distant planet known to the ancients, Saturn is surrounded by rings, a natural symbol for the farthest limits of consciousness. We may say that Saturn is that factor in human consciousness which sets up boundaries, which establishes limits for us. These limits can be positive, as when we limit our indulgences or our bad habits. But more often, it is something bright and "shining"—something akin to the magic world of a man's interior Grail Castle—which becomes imprisoned within those rings.

Let us consider yet another aspect of Saturn. Medieval Christians identified this planet with the Devil, whom they imagined as a wild, horned beast. In astrology, Saturn rules the sign Capricorn, often equated with the god Pan, that feral, unabashedly sexual god of the woods.[7] In one sense, then, gloomy Saturn shows us another, unexpected face: that of the Wild Man who, like Bran, partakes of the primal energy of earth and sea, of the Children of Llyr.

It is this feral, pagan man who is trapped within our self-made walls. It is their wildness, their spontaneity and creativity which men are all too likely to imprison within the iron-clad rings of Saturn, establishing boundaries and limits which orient them exclusively towards the world of material reality (Saturn's realm, according to astrology).

To create or impose upon ourselves such limitations is a natural consequence of opening the original wound—in a sense, these limitations constitute the wound itself. We take our first tentative steps into the world while still under the dreamy spell of the Grail Castle. But the world all too quickly disillusions us. We are forced to hide our childlike magic, our prancing Wild Man, so that the world will not notice us—which is to say, so that we shall not be hurt or wounded further. We don a more anonymous (and, in our own society, quite literal) suit of gray, for we are unable to bear the pain which ensues when our childhood grail world collides with the colder, darker world of Saturn. Little by little, we bid farewell to the Otherworld—the unified womb-world of the mother. We move, albeit reluctantly, into the world of the father—for Saturn is a father symbol as well. We have boundaried our wound—our bright and shining essence—with a castle of iron.

But if we are now protected in a suit of armor and thus able to play the Warrior's role in earnest, we have also established for ourselves a spiritual isolation. After all, there is nothing quite so lonely as being imprisoned in a castle or an armored suit. The grail world, almost by definition, connected us with everything in the universe.

The wound, again by definition, isolates us from that universe. And Saturn, to astrologers, is the planet of isolation. We have learned to play one role, to walk one path. It may be the path of the Warrior, Lover, Magician, or King. But it is a solitary path all the same.

We have spoken of discrimination—the masculine ability to *separate* one thing from another. This discriminative function—our masculine sword—is one of the inner psychological factors which differentiates us from women. We *need* our swords of separation, for a lack of discrimination has gotten many a male hero into serious trouble. The Norse god Tyr lost a hand trying to tame the fierce Fenris wolf. But the task of discrimination and differentiation, the path of awakened mind or logos, is a lonely path. Discrimination equals isolation.

The man who has turned his back upon his perfect Grail moments and entered Saturn's gray world has placed his Wild Man in a cage. Without the sustaining power of that vital pagan force, his isolation may well equal desperation. The world comes to be perceived as profane rather than sacred; and indeed, for most men the workaday world is profane. We have been forced to perform like automatons, bound and gagged by convention and by conformity to the whims of an increasingly immoral majority. The isolationist becomes a member of his own moral minority by virtue of his walls, seeking unity within himself. Even his return from the office, construction site, or gas station, back to home and family, may leave him with a feeling of solitary confinement just as powerful as that which haunts him on the job—especially if his marriage is less than perfect. Women (wives in particular) often seem to favor men who are sufficiently disciplined enough to go out and earn the paycheck, who can be big car-fixing galoots in their spare time, but who are nevertheless under the total domination and control of their women! No wonder Al Bundy, the hopeless shoe salesman on the TV sitcom *Married With Children,* has been a popular male archetype for almost a decade. Sometimes men just want to retreat from themselves and everything around them.

The Grail myth catches this isolation perfectly in the symbol of the wasteland. Because of the Fisher King's painful wound, all the land about the Grail Castle has become barren. It no longer bears fruit. It no longer has juice and vitality. The same may be said of a man who has closed off his inner shining self, his Cernunnos, and donned his figurative suit of armored gray. He has learned to function perfectly in the world of the father, but his spirit is barren, isolated, laid waste. He can achieve but he cannot create—not until he comes again, perhaps in the middle of his life, to the Grail Castle, and asks the right questions.

As we can see, it is both incorrect and decidedly unkind to assume that sex is the basic root of the male "problem" and applicable to *all* men. Unfortunately, many women of the staunch New Age variety fall into this trap and, in their own quest for completion, may actually regard symbolic castration as a viable alternative to bring about equality of the sexes. (Ouch!) This lack of respect for a man's Warrior spirit has resulted in what Robert Bly calls the "soft male." This term is not a too-literal reference to a flaccid erection; rather, Bly is describing a man who has been initiated primarily by women and who has therefore learned to be a sensitive, nurturing caretaker of home, family, and earth—but who has lost the divine spark or Wild Man within himself.[8] As with the self-isolated Warrior, it is the Wild Man who is likely to become a victim when the soft man, initiated by women, takes over as the principal factor in a man's personality. But this emasculation is what both women and society seem to expect of a man these days. (Not surprisingly, many men—even the "soft" types—assume a defensive posture against this ferocious assault on their manhood, and may thus perpetuate the medieval concept of woman as the "weaker sex" in an attempt to repair their battered egos and regain their lost strength.) Because we live in a world of "soft" men—and, to be perfectly honest, the men who read books on mythology and spirituality such as this one tend to be in that category—it may be worth our while to ask how such a man takes shape. What is his story?

A young man, an adolescent, whose spirit still lingers in the Grail Castle of childhood, is unaware of his inner wounds—if, in fact, he has yet acquired any. He is still part of a perfect unity which is the unity of unconsciousness, the unity of the womb. Such a man—or, more properly, such a boy—is still tied to the mother, and cannot, under such circumstances, truly become a man. The

The Wounded Fisher King

primal unity of the feminine is not at all the same thing as the spiritual unity of the mature, self-aware man. This is why the Grail Castle must be lost and then regained. This is why Perceval must be wrenched away from his mother—made conscious of her death—in order to have his wound rightly opened and be cast out of the childhood grail world.

Many boys would rather not leave that first, most wondrous of all Grail Castles. Why face battle, why be wounded, why walk a lonely path through life only to regain, later on, what is already there at the beginning? Better not to leave. Better to stay wrapped in the golden ecstasy of childhood.

Such men never become fully awake and adult. They may be brilliant—in fact, a great number of the poets and musicians of the world are in this category. Such a child-man seeks to soar into the realms of spirit, to fly high toward the infinite and thus escape the horrible wounds that should awaken his adult self. (Some psychologists call this type of boy-man the *puer aeternus,* or eternal child.) Bly calls him "the flying boy" because he strives, like Icarus, to soar into the heart of the sun. Like the boy in Bly's well-known interpretation of the "Iron John" fairy tale, his hair has turned to gold but he has not yet learned to put a cap over his glory, a protective covering that will allow him to face the world. He still shines with the glow of his grail experience. Hence he may long to devote his life to poetry, to love. He may take up the "spiritual quest" at an early age, long before he has mastered this world. Sadly, his quest for ecstasy and love is in reality a staunch refusal to abandon the world of the mother, the divine feminine. This is why his quest is doomed to failure. A man cannot fly through the air until he has learned to place his feet on the ground. And he cannot be firmly rooted in the ground unless he is rooted with blood and tears, the rewards of his inner wound.[9]

This scenario would seem to make the Great Mother into a bit of a villainess. We are reminded that, in many mythologies, the Great Mother not only nurtures, she also devours. Is it true, then, that men feel threatened by the female of the species? Or do women really hold the key which will unlock the vital life-giving energy which so many modern men feel is lacking in themselves?

The Iron John fairy tale places the hairy Wild Man inside an iron cage, and Bly tells us that the key to the cage—and hence to a man's inner nature—must be retrieved from a woman. Not just retrieved, but stolen. No easy task for the king's five-year-old son, who has lost his golden ball in the hairy man's cage and can only regain it by releasing the Wild Man from his prison. The key to the Wild Man's cage is in the possession of the queen—the boy's mother, of course—who keeps it under her pillow.[10]

Just as this theft is no easy task for the little boy, neither is it easy for the gentle, sensitive man of the nineties, who would rather not think about *stealing* the key, even if it's the key to his own soul. It is a job which requires the courage of one's convictions—and sufficient self-motivation to act in willful disobedience to the apparent source of one's sustenance and survival. Tricking the Great Mother is a tricky business indeed.

Perceval found himself in somewhat the same situation during his first visit to the Grail Castle. He was afraid to steal the key to the Grail mystery by asking questions. Fortunately for Perceval, this didn't stop him. He continued his quest. But what would have happened to him had he turned back, refused to seek the answers? What happens to little boys who refuse to steal the key?

When a man hangs back from his inner motivations, dreams and desires, he can only act in overtly negative and extreme ways, usually directed against that which he perceives to be the source of his hurt, his sadness, shame, guilt, or confusion, the numbness and emptiness he feels as a result of being separated from the vital inner Self. For most men, whether traditional macho types or soft-style New Agers, these "ways" are *other*-destructive as well as *self*-destructive. Men tend to project their anger while at the same time denying or seeming to be unconscious of those very projections, unconscious of their actions and of the internal frustration and rage which produces those actions. Thus violence (whether against women or other men), psychological abuse, alcoholism and other forms of chemical dependence, workaholism, sex addiction, co-dependence, rageaholism, incest, mental and physical illness and, finally, suicide are on the rise as fear-based reactions to feelings of grief and despair, collective as well as individual. Fear as a root emotion is the same for men and women alike. The proverbial battle of the sexes is due to our fear—our fear of change and our fear of the unknown. We all want love; we all crave that others will willingly accept our frailties. People do not consciously set out to be tried, judged, and hung, whether by a jury of their peers or by the opposite sex.

All this discussion about the sacred wound in its various manifestations has perhaps led us to one central truth: at root, male woundedness stems from a fear of being *vulnerable* (the feeling function or Grail) and/or *ineffectual* (the sensation function or dish) rather than from mere sexual inadequacy. In order to demonstrate their prowess as Kings, Lovers, Warriors, or Magicians in terms of *action*, men need to strive consciously for *perfection* in the outer world while simultaneously seeking to unleash the Wild Man and discover the Higher Self asleep within the personal ego.

Now perhaps we can reach for a better understanding of why the "sacred wound" so often strikes a man in the thighs. One cannot be mobile or physically active in the outside world without the use of the thighs. The thighs are the prop or support for the entire body, a symbol of *strength*. The thighs enable man to walk in an upright position, as only humans can do. (Anthropologists have correlated the ability to stand upright and the general development of the spinal column with the potential for evolutionary growth.) Astrology associates the thighs with the sign Sagittarius and the planet Jupiter, and thereby with a whole range of symbolic meanings that include expansiveness, optimism, prosperity, generosity, and truthfulness.

Sometimes, as we have seen, the wound occurs in the heel or foot rather than the thigh. If we consider the foot through astrological symbolism, we find ourselves in the realm of Pisces, the fish. And though contemporary astrologers would link Pisces with the planet Neptune, their medieval counterparts would have attributed it to Jupiter, the same planet which is archetypally associated with the thigh! (Jupiter was, of course, the *king* of the gods, and most of our "wounded heroes" are either kings or warriors.) Carrying our search further, we may note that in the most ancient times the fish was in fact linked with the thigh rather than the foot.

The frozen, and hence perfectly preserved, body of a Scythian shaman discovered in Siberia revealed a man entirely covered with tatoos. Upon the shaman's thigh was etched the image of a fish. Interpreting the shaman's tatoos, Hungarian linguist Otto Sadovsky argued that the fish was anciently regarded as the "prop of the universe," a symbol which persisted into Christian times when Christ himself was linked with the fish.[11]

Among the Celts, the fish was linked with the Otherworld and its wisdom, that which lies beneath the surface of appearances. Jung informs us that in alchemy the fish came to be seen as a symbol of the Self dwelling in the unconscious mind, because the fish dwells in the deep waters which symbolize the unconscious in so many different traditions.[12]

Instinctual and automatic in its responses to the world, the unconscious is amenable to our control only via *suggestion*—thus the wise man, the Druid or Magician, is he who is the master of such suggestions. But all of us must, at one time or another, play the Magician's role, employing subtletly and stealth when swimming through the uncharted depths of the primordial ocean—lest we encounter sea monsters or seductive mermaids who compel us to relinquish our conscious control to all that is primitive, wild, unknown. In order to heal their wounds, men must go swimming in the fearsome undersea lands, hoping to catch the fish of the Self in the process. And along with death and taxes, one more thing is certain: someday we must face the shadow side of our own nature. Someday the sea-monsters and mermaids will shape-change into all our negative characteristics, the projected violence and addictive "isms" described above. The primal brain is the cage that holds the Wild Man—he who is our weakness, our frailty and vulnerability as well as our strength, our virility, and our very life-force.

To be wounded in the thigh or heel is to lose the support of the unconscious. Without its sustaining power, we are unable to navigate through the dark waters of the soul. We can no longer see the Self, glowing like a luminous fish in the depths of the sea. The sacred wound, then, may at last be understood as symbolic of a man's inability to grow in spiritual knowledge and understanding unless he comes to realize the Higher Self as the only genuine support for his quest.

But if the sacred wound of the Fisher King is the festering sore which isolates men from the universe around them, then why is it also an initiation? Why is the wound the worldwide prerequisite for those who would take the shaman's path? This brings us back to Bran son of Llyr.

Bran's magic wound, the spear in his heel, is fatal. His brother Manawyddan lops his head off, but not before receiving Bran's final instructions. The dying king instructs his surviving companions to bear his severed head to the White Hill near London, but by a most circuitous route. First the companions of Bran are to cross the sea from Ireland to Harlech in North Wales. There, in Harlech, they will feast for seven years, listening to the magic singing of the birds of Rhiannon. Then they are to proceed to South Wales, where their magic feasting will last a full eighty years—until one of them opens the door of the mead hall and breaks the spell.

The heroes obey the last wishes of Bran. For eighty-seven years they enjoy a magic feast in a magic hall. This may remind us of those Celtic heroes who visit the world of the fairies and lose themselves in the "hollow hills" for a night which proves to last a hundred years, but it should also remind us of the Grail Castle. Bran is still among his companions, even though as a severed head (perhaps on a serving dish?). He speaks to his friends, and, in the words of the *Mabinogion*, is "as pleasant company to them as when their lord had been alive." Afterwards, his head is buried on that hill near London, to serve as a vehicle of prophecy for all England.[13]

Clearly, then, Bran's passage into death has opened up for him a whole new dimension. Is this myth a metaphor for the inner, spiritual death which opens new vistas of consciousness, such as the ability to prophesy? A Greek myth tells us how Chiron, the wise king of the centaurs, was wounded in the heel (or thigh) by a poisoned arrow. Unable to die because he was immortal, he simply lingered in pain. Finally, he *chose* to die. But his dying had a higher purpose: the gods had once decreed that Prometheus, the divine rebel who stole the fire of enlightenment to give to humankind, could only be released from his prison on the mountaintop if one of the immortals were to die. This seemingly impossible condition was fulfilled by Chiron's death. Prometheus, symbol of fiery enlightenment, returned to humankind.[14]

This drama of death and transformation brings us back to alchemy, which, we may remember, has symbolic links with Bran by way of his totems, the crow and raven. The initial stages of the alchemical process, like the knight's classic quest, are solitary. We must all become Lone Rangers as regards fixing the wagon of our personal selves. Alchemy as a psychological process aims at a state of consciousness which manifests in the world as perfect balance. This is only possible through a complete regeneration of the personality, a deepened understanding of life founded upon inner experience. The *nigredo* phase of the journey is often described in terms of "self-putrefaction"—the decomposition or breakdown of the personality into elementary components. But once the ego structure has been dissolved and gently submerged in the dark waters of the collective unconscious, it rises again through a process the alchemists called "sublimation." At this stage mind and spirit become energized, bringing a clear vision which is in harmony with the whole universe and which may be defined as "enlightenment" in the Eastern sense of the word. Equilibrium is maintained by the universal life-force flowing through us in an unobstructed manner—unhindered by a purely personal will or complex of desires. False opinions have been annihilated during the *nigredo,* a transformation which catapults us out of denial and into a consciousness of the Self. This transformation has repercussions for all our relationships as well as for ourselves. Certainly the advent of prophecy brings Bran—even after death—into a more powerful sense of relationship with his people; i.e., the collective. In more intimate relationships as well, the alchemical process is fundamental—in a sense, alchemy may be said to be primarily "about" the tempering of relationships. Only a man who has passed through the Saturnian darkness of the *nigredo* can fully realize the alchemy of the sexes.

Here we see clearly the real drama of the sacred wound, one which lies implicit in the story of Bran or the Fisher King, but which is all too confused in Celtic myth—perhaps because the

Celtic traditions were more severely tampered with by Christians than were the Greek. The wound is that which makes us aware of the great gulf between our shining, inner grail world and the cold outer world of responsibility. No wonder, then, that the wound is magic: it introduces men to the searing tension of the opposites, makes them aware that there are two worlds, one of matter and one of spirit. We hide our shining Grail King within ourselves, and with him vanishes his darker, animal brother, Cernunnos the Wild Man. Now we are entirely and completely isolated. But this isolation, this consciousness of duality and human suffering, is a necessary thing, for no one can become a shaman, a Druid, or a prophet without such an understanding. One who remains locked in his suit of armor or his childhood castle will never attain the stature of consciousness, the compassion which only comes with a knowledge of human suffering. It is this knowledge of duality, this compassion, which makes it possible for a man to become a prophet or a wise man.

All men are wounded. Some are born with their wounds, while most incur them during childhood or adolescence. All of us have a predisposition to be wounded and to deny our wounds well into adulthood.

There are many different kinds of wounds. Each of the four paths of male initiation has its own specific wound.

The Warrior, in his attempts to show courage, initiative, and bravado, is prone to fits of impatience, willfulness, and violence. He will do anything to get what he wants, even if he must use force or threats.

Sometimes the Lover will act out in a similar manner as a result of feeling inadequate or ineffectual in the outside world. But in general, the Lover's wound becomes apparent in his relationships with women. He will be emotional, over-sensitive, and insecure, possessing an inaccurate and inhibiting sense of self. There may be a self-indulgent attitude in his dealings with the opposite sex. He may be demanding and greedy, making uncomfortable emotional demands on his partner. Contrary to the generosity of spirit which should permeate this archetype, he may turn cold, his affections inhibited. The "soft" male often manifests some of these traits, and is often in denial concerning his actions and responses to others. He may resort to negative escapism and become evasive regarding commitment or any sense of responsibility to the self's deepest needs.

The Magician is a wily creature, like the Native American Coyote, and this makes it difficult to recognize his wound. When he is engaged in action, he may misuse his skill or intelligence. This is the amoral man who is able to rationalize anything. He is often opinionated or one-sided in his efforts to communicate. The passive Magician, on the other hand, lacks faith in others and is thus limited because he depends upon himself for everything. He may be rigid, cold, defensive, and display fearfulness and negativity at the slightest provocation.

The wound of the King, when negatively expressed, manifests as pride, arrogance, and an excessive desire to be "special." Men wounded in this manner may be overconfident or lazy, scattering their energy in too many directions and leaving their work to be completed by others. They may show irresponsibility by overextending themselves and promising others either too little or too much. Kings, like Warriors, are willful, restless, and impatient. They require excitement and sometimes purposeless change, and they are apt to become either rebellious or tyrannical when making important decisions.

These psychological sketches of male woundedness are but surface manifestations. The real wound at the heart of things stems from the shadow side of the self. Everyone has a Shadow. It rises up from the depths of our unconscious when we are unable to accept the need to focus our minds and will power towards our own transformation. The Shadow may rob us of the courage to face our deepest desires and compulsions and to transmute them through effort and intense experience. The Shadow may lead us to the compulsive expression of unconscious motivations and desires. Sometimes it leads to the willful manipulation of others in order to serve our own ends. When the dark side of the sacred wound is in full flower, a man may become ruthless and infatuated with power in an attempt to avoid the pain of facing himself.

In order to heal our Shadow, and thus make the Grail King's inner realm flourish and bloom again, we must, as we have seen by now, release the Wild Man from within his gray castle walls—for it is he, at one with all Nature, who can restore the wasteland to its natural state.

But how shall we accomplish this?

Notes

1. Robert Johnson, *He*, 12.

2. Ibid.

3. Gantz, *Mabinogion*, 66–82.

4. Ibid., 217–57.

5. Graves, *The White Goddess*, 52.

6. Jung and von Franz, *The Grail Legend*, 205.

7. Ariel Guttman and Kenneth Johnson, *Mythic Astrology: Archetypal Powers in the Horoscope* (St. Paul, MN: Llewellyn, 1993), 334–5.

8. Bly, *Iron John*, 2–4.

9. Ibid., 57–67.

10. Ibid., 10–12.

11. Personal communication with the author, 1971.

12. Jung, *Aion: Researches into the Phenomenology of the Self* (Collected Works, vol. 9, part II) (Princeton: Princeton University Press, 1970), 72–172.

13. Gantz, *Mabinogion*, 81.

14. Guttman and Johnson, *Mythic Astrology*, 141–50.

CHAPTER 12

The Enlightenment of Finn MacCool

Many writers, throughout the Middle Ages, sought many and various solutions to the Grail mystery. More often than not, however, they were unable to find within themselves the answer to the most vital question:

How shall the Grail King be healed?

Perhaps it is not terribly surprising that the Grail Legend begins to falter precisely here, at the most important point. As Jung pointed out, the writers of the Grail stories were, whether consciously or unconsciously, sounding a grave warning concerning the direction which Western civilization was taking. But the course of history was rushing on at such a rapid pace that the solution—if indeed there was one—seemed to blow away on the winds of change.

From this greater distance, however, we may at least seek a few clues. Let us begin by returning to Perceval's experience upon leaving the Grail Castle for the first time. He was confronted by an angry woman who took him severely to task for not asking the relevant questions.

One of these questions, and the one which turns up most often in the later Grail literature, was this one:

Whom does the Grail serve?

The answer, according to several medieval sources, is that the Grail serves the Grail King. He must drink of the Cauldron of the Goddess, the Cauldron of Rebirth, for it is from this always brimming vessel that the Otherworld Queen has filled her great goblet, the cup she holds forth to all those who reach those wild and misty realms.

But what, precisely, glimmers in her cup? It is not enough to say simply that it is the substance or the power of rebirth and rejuvenation, for that in itself will not help *us* to drink from its depths.

Throughout the world of Indo-European myth, there are numerous examples of the "food of the gods" which makes the immortals what they are—immortal. The Vedic gods of India were dependent upon a magical substance called *amrita* to maintain their immortality. This same word appears in Greek myth as *ambrosia,* the substance which bestowed eternal life and youth upon the gods of Olympus. This ambrosia was served to the gods in a cup held by the goddess Hebe—yet another incarnation of the Brigid or Rhiannon who, in Celtic myth, is keeper of the sacred cauldron.

A related concept from Vedic myth is that of *soma,* a mysterious magical drink which bestows ecstasy as well as rejuvenation. The Greeks recognized mead as such a drink, sacred to Dionysus, and among the Vikings it was mead which bestowed upon a man the gift of poetic inspiration.

The drink called soma originated with an herb or plant. Some scholars have tried to idenitfy it with a real botanical plant, notably the fly agaric or magic mushroom. Others have insisted that the soma is metaphorical rather than real. What is more important to our purposes is the fact that the Vedic hymns *perceive* it as a real herb which must be gathered like any other, but which has the power to heal all illnesses:

> *In Soma's realm are many herbs,*
> *And knowledge a hundredfold have they,*

Of all these herbs thou art the best
The wish to fulfill and heart to heal....

May he who plants you know no harm,
Nor he for whom your seed is sown!
With us shall all, both man and beast,
Well and free from danger be.

All you who listen to my word,
You who are far away from here,
All you plants unite together,
And grant your strength to this one herb![1]

It is as such that the magical healing herb appears in the Grail Legend. Chretien de Troyes tells us that Sir Gawain, upon spying a wounded knight lying by the road, heals him thus:

To make the sick knight thrive,
A herb to cure all pain
That in a hedge had lain
He spied, and thence he plucked it.[2]

The theme of the Grail Knight as magical healer was first articulated by the British scholar Jessie L. Weston, who, in 1920, published a book entitled *From Ritual to Romance*. This study of the Grail Legend—which found the origins of the myth in ancient fertility rituals—was hotly debated and finally dismissed by most scholars. The book, however, was highly influential in a literary sense, for it helped give birth to T.S. Eliot's famous poem "The Waste Land." In our opinion, Weston raised many extremely valid points, not least among them the references to the Grail Knight as healer. She points out that it is inevitably Sir Gawain, rather than any of King Arthur's other knights, who is the master healer, and that he appears in this role rather often. Furthermore, the tradition is an ancient one. In the old poems known as the Welsh Triads, the knight Gwalchmai appears as a healer, and Gwalchmai (Hawk of May) is the old Welsh equivalent of Gawain. The Triads name only one other knight after this fashion: Peredur is called "chief healer." Peredur, of course, is equivalent to Pryderi and to Perceval, so that in any event the role of the healer is vested in the Grail Knight rather than in any other figure.[3]

It may be well to note here that magical healing, especially with herbs, is one of the principal activities of the shaman. It is a bit frustrating to find so little information concerning the nature of Gawain's magic herb, though Weston also discovered a reference to Arthur's knights discovering an herb "which belonged to the Grail."[4] This is an important clue, for it links the healing herb with the substance in the grail cup, but we have not yet identified the substance which we ourselves must "drink" in order to restore the wounded King within us all.

We have seen that the Greek goddess Hebe, like the queen of the Celtic Otherworld, offered up ambrosia to the gods to make them immortal. But she is not the only goddess who has the magic of eternal youth in her keeping. The Viking sagas attribute the same role to the goddess Idun, who keeps the apples of eternal youth in a bowl or basket. We are never told, in so many words, where these apples come from, but we may remember that Celtic voyagers to the Otherworld often encountered a great tree there, and that the birds of the Goddess sang in that tree. The husband of Idun was Bragi, god of poetry and inspiration, and to the Norse the winning of poetic inspiration was a gift of the sacred mead—which, as we have seen, is yet another metaphor for the food of the gods.

The World Tree may be an ash, a yew, a hazel, or a birch. It may be any kind of tree at all. But at its feet, in ancient times, a goddess waited, with basket, cup, or cauldron brimming with the fruit, the essence, of the great Tree itself. The World Tree, the Tree of Life, had its branches in heaven and its roots in hell. From its roots or at its base flowed streams of pure, life-giving water which formed pools or wells—Norse myth recognizes a Well of Memory and a Well of Fate. The Judeo-Christian tradition "splits" the World Tree by postulating *two* trees—a Tree of Life and a Tree of the Knowledge of Good and Evil. The god Yahweh invited Adam and Eve to eat of the Tree of Life, but forbade them the Tree of the Knowledge of Good and Evil. Enlightenment, in Judeo-Christian terms, consists of turning one's vital energies inward, away from the dangerous knowledge of worldly wisdom and sword-wielding dualities. Pagan enlightenment, on the other hand, consists of tasting the fruit of the Tree which is *both* Life and Knowledge, and letting the juice run down one's chin. There is a story from Celtic myth which illustrates this quality of pagan enlightenment, and teaches us what a man must do, and the qualities he must cultivate, in order to attain it. That story is the story of Finn MacCool's enlightenment, his journey to the heart of the Grail Castle where he tasted of the Tree of Life itself and drank deep of the cauldron of inspiration.

In Chapter 7, we received a glimpse of the old Celtic World Tree. When King Cormac arrived in the Otherworld kingdom of Manannan mac Lir, the first thing he saw was this:

> ...*a shining fountain, with five streams flowing out of it, and the hosts in turn drinking its water. Nine hazels of Buan grew over the well. The purple hazels dropped their nuts into the fountain, and the five salmon which were in the fountain severed them and sent their husks floating down the streams.*[5]

This is the World Tree, imaged here as *nine* trees, to which Finn paid a momentous visit.

Finn MacCool was one of the great heroes of pagan Ireland. A war leader rather than a king, he lived in the wilderness with his band of warriors, all of them sworn to protect the sacred land of Ireland. When one of Finn's heroes wandered off to the Land of Youth, he returned to Ireland to find his comrades all dead and the Christians in charge. St. Patrick tried to convert the old warrior, telling him that his companions were surely burning in hell rather than feasting in any pagan Otherworld. But the old man firmly told the saint:

> ...*when life in my body has ceased,*
> *I will go to Caoilte, and Conan, and Bran, Sceolan, Lomair,*
> *And dwell in the house of the Fenians, be they in flames or at feast.*[6]

The last of the Fenians preferred the flames of the Christian hell to the notion of being separated from his warrior companions. This fierce devotion to one's comrades and to the land itself lived on in Ireland long after the time of Finn—the original members of the Irish Republican Army called themselves Fenians, for they believed that they were fighting in the spirit of Finn MacCool just as surely as some modern-day American Indians believe that they are fighting in the spirit of Crazy Horse.

But Finn himself, like most heroes, was a lonely and abandoned child. The son of a war leader slain in battle, Finn was taken into the forest by his mother in order to protect him from his father's enemies. He was given the name of Demne and reared, as we have noted, by two "warrior women," Bodball the Druidess and the Gray One of Luachar. In time he won the name of Finn, the "fair one" or "white one," but kept the name of Demne when first he left the forest to begin his adventures.

One of these adventures[7] was the acquisition of knowledge, and specifically of poetry—the old tale informs us that he had to learn poetry on account of his father's enemies.

Finn, still calling himself Demne, went to the cottage of an old bard, also called Finn, who lived by a pool on the River Boyne. He had lived there for many a year, for it had been prophesied that a man named Finn would eat the salmon of knowledge. The old bard believed himself to be that Finn. But what was the salmon of knowledge?

On the Boyne, it is said, was a great hazel tree, and below it a pool of water which gave birth to a stream and flowed, in time, into the Boyne. The hazel tree dropped its nuts into the pool, where they were eaten by an old salmon. Here, then, is the Celtic World Tree which lies at the center of the Grail Castle mandala, and the hazel nuts are yet another metaphor for the food of the gods, that which grants us both youth and inspiration. The pool in which the salmon swims is equivalent to the Norse Well of Memory or Fate—or perhaps to both of those famous pools.

The elder Finn, however, had not yet succeeded in capturing the salmon. He decided to let his apprentice Demne do the hard work of fishing, though he told the youth: "Only *catch* and then *cook* the salmon. Do not *eat* of it."

Finn MacCool and the Salmon

Young Finn set to work and caught the fish. He put it in a skillet and began dutifully to fry it up. But the grease splattered, as grease will do, and burned his thumb. Finn quickly placed his thumb in his mouth, beneath a tooth, in order to cool it.

And at that moment, or so we may assume, all knowledge and all wisdom burst upon him.

Still doing his duty, the youth—who was a youth no longer—brought the cooked salmon to his master. But the old man must have seen something new and shining in the young apprentice, for he asked of him:

"Did you eat any of this fish, boy?"

And Finn told him what had happened.

"Well, then," said the old man, "your name too must be Finn, and the salmon is yours. Go ahead and eat it."

Finn ate the salmon, and from that time on he had only to place his thumb upon his tooth in order to gain access to all the poetry, magic, and knowledge he would ever need.

When we taste the oil of the salmon of knowledge—when we drink from the Grail—we sate our desires, soothe our souls, and quench our burning thirst for more. We reach conclusion, completion, and enlightenment because we can no longer be selfish in our needs and wants. Our senses are open to the knowledge, wisdom, and understanding of all creatures and things. We are grown in compassion and devotion to lving gods and goddesses who abide in everything in the world around us: the sun, the moon, the sky, the earth, the air, the water, in trees and meadows, in creatures of all dimensions and varieties, and, at once, in ourselves.

It may strike some of us as curious that the legend creates the equation poetry = knowledge. The term "poetry" has a decidedly "soft" feeling for most of us and signifies a highly refined, perhaps effete brand of literature practiced by timorous, over-sensitive souls. But this is *not* the kind of poetry Finn is hoping to practice. Let us remember that he *had* to learn the art of poetry "on account of his father's enemies." Poetry, then, was a magic power, a kind of strength which would nurture his soul and protect his body.

The term "poetry" would have signified a great power indeed to the old Celtic Druids—a power so great as to constitute a weapon. When the ancient Celts went into battle, each army had its Druids standing nearby to sing and chant spells, poems of power which were capable of stopping enemy forces in their tracks, or raising a fog of confusion in which men might become lost. This brand of poetry, then, is a fire in the soul, a great *force* rather than a mere literary pastime. It is the fire of inspiration signified by mead. It is the life, the magic and vitality in a man's soul.

How, then, does a man cultivate "poetry in the soul?" He need not actually sit down and *write* anything—though it would certainly be a good idea if more men were to set down their impressions of the world around them. Poetry is a good, strong habit, not a sissified indulgence. It brings a man into contact with his own deepest thoughts, feelings, and desires in a way that few other disciplines can do. But the essential way to find the poetry in one's own soul is to journey (as often as possible) to the depths of one's being, and to look out upon the world from that vantage point.

Before our ideas can emerge into the physical world, they must first be purified in the deep waters of the unconscious—that realm of fluctuating emotions, feelings, responses, and memories. It is from this deep well that our sensations of intuition and compassion arise. Within this world of desire, form and force are united. The watery essence of mind is also the wellspring of our sexual nature and hence the surge of our passions. It is through this area of consciousness, the dwelling-place of those archetypes we call "feminine" or "lunar," that a man may understand the complex of essential qualities inherent in his own feminine side—and in the women of this world as well. By tapping into his instinctual, primal self, he may become aware of the Warrior, Lover, Magician, and King who fight or love or create or rule in order to fulfill the circumstances of his own life experience. He may also—regardless of his actual age—become aware of the strong naked youth who yet lives inside. Time does not exist in the Otherworld.

The silent flame of hidden wisdom feeds our intuition, and from the contemplative mood thus engendered springs inspiration. However, it is the vital sense of purpose and well-being, the creativity, authority, and pride in one's individuality, that brings inspiration to life. With this comes balance and harmony between the light and dark forces within a man's soul. Fear comes when there is only a reflected light to guide us on the path. The draught from the Cauldron of Rebirth, the water of wisdom which burns with the fire of the sun, washes away fear, rigidity, caution, and inhibition. Old thoughts and habit patterns that are no longer useful are swept away and beyond remembrance. Our tongues are numbed by the aged brew and our minds alerted to the call of imagination, dream, the music of the soul.

In ancient times, European shamans might have mixed for us authentic potions, perhaps containing such herbs as mandrake, damiana, almond, hazel, moonwort, poppy, hibiscus, or nettle. The healing balm in these ancient, wisdom-giving herbs brought relief to the troubled mind by soothing the frantic, restless voices that serve no real purpose in the fulfillment of our destiny. Drinking deep of our own grail, we too may be quieted, silenced, and thus enabled to listen with our hearts. No longer abiding in dark, shadowy places, blinded by light's reflection, we may now gaze fully awake, alert and alive, into the face of the sky. Cernunnos, god of the Earth and the Otherworld just beyond and beneath it, dances with pagan Diana, the Celtic Arianrhod, goddess of the Silver Wheel. Both move in harmony to the rhythms of the natural world, our Earth.

Finn had to catch the salmon in order to attain that fire. We have noted earlier that the fish is an emblem of the Self—the luminous essence of our individuality which swims beneath the surface of our lives, in the well of the unconscious. We must plunge deep into the unconscious, make the Otherworld journey, if we are to capture that fish. The Grail King is a Fisher King, for he too seeks the Self, the only thing that can make him whole. To drink the mead of inspiration which gleams in the Grail cup is to catch the fish of the Self.

Though the Otherworld journey to the Grail Castle is important, it is not the whole story. More to the point, it needs a context. We live in a psychological civilization. We have been brought up to believe that the journey is entirely an *inward* thing. We study our "issues," analyze ourselves and our parents, and perhaps become endlessly lost in such introverted speculations. We no longer face outward, towards the world. We seek the Grail Castle, that sense of unity and oneness with the universe which is our inheritance as human beings, entirely within ourselves.

This path will never lead a man to wholeness. It will only lead him back to the womb. For Finn, after his poetic enlightenment, after the awakening of the fire in his soul, did not shield himself in some internal Grail Castle of meditation and contemplation. He returned to the world; he became a Warrior once again.

And yet he is no longer the lonely, wounded Warrior who wanders lost through the depths of a forest of isolation. For now he sees the Otherworldly glow of the grail world *everywhere*, in everything around him. Most importantly, he sees it in *Nature*, for the Pan or Cernunnos within him is alive once again.

Here is the poem he made after his enlightenment experience:

> May Day, the best of all seasons, vibrant with color!
> The blackbirds sing their songs in full,
> as long as there is light to sing.
> The dusty cuckoo calls the summer in,
> Summer free of bitterness, greening every wood.
>
> Horses swiftly seek the river, flowing smoothly now.
> The heather spreads her long hair,
> The soft white bog-fern grows.
> The deer leaps high with startled heart
> And the ocean storms subside;
> The sea is smooth, the world is rich with blossoming.
> The bees are small but carry burdens great and sweet;
> The stag tracks mud up hillside and the ants are at their
>   feasts.
> The forest tunes its harp; sails billow on the lakes....
> Birds settle in the meadow; the green fields whisper and
>   the white streams roar.
> You long to race on horses swift and see the armies gather.
> An arrow of sunlight strikes the land and sparks the gold
>   beneath.
> The lark is singing like a small wild fool,
> For May Day of delicate color.[8]

Finn glories in the celebration of Nature, pure and simple. It is the natural world of trees, meadows, and birdsong that now glows with the Otherworldly light of the Grail Castle.

And this, finally, is the secret of "poetry in the soul." It is a way of *seeing*.

Born in the bright womb of the grail, we set forth upon our individual journeys into manhood. When we become sick and weary of the quest, we take the shaman's journey to the Otherworld. If we are to gain from that journey, it must become part of us—we must bear some of the Otherworldly wisdom back into *this* world with us.

This is not easy. Celtic heroes of myth and folklore often find themselves stranded once again in an everyday world, with only a lingering sense of music and delight to remind them that, once upon a time, they too tasted the fruit of the great hazel tree. If we are to take up our quest again, fully alive and empowered and ready to work for the good of the tribe—or, in more contemporary terms, of the planet—we need more than a little bit of lingering music.

We need constantly to be reminded that the world—all the creatures and people in it—do indeed glow with a divine light. This knowledge, this vision, is our inheritance from the Otherworld, the Grail Castle. To cleanse our vision and perceive a world of light is to drink of the mead of inspiration and heal the Grail King. The wasteland is waste no longer; it is paradise.

We may remember that the Grail King's pain became more intense at the time of Saturn's rising and the new moon. Wolfram von Eschenbach tells us that the King could only find relief if the magic spear of the Grail was placed against his wound. When we discussed the Magician (Chapter 4), we learned that the spear, among other things, symbolizes successful struggle. It is a symbol of energy and renewal as well as of creativity. But even more significantly for our purposes, the spear is a phallic symbol.

And yet did we not say that the Fisher King's wound is *not* inherently sexual? What, then, does the Grail King's penis have to do with his kingdom laid to waste and the healing of his body and soul? Are we contradicting ourselves?

Indeed, in one important sense the King's wound is not sexual, for the average man doesn't *really* spend his time worrying about whether his tool will work properly or whether he can use it to gain power over women, as so many would have us believe. The Grail King's wound, however, has a curious relationship to sexuality because, as we have seen, it is his very life-force which is wounded, and sexuality powers the life force—according to many occult systems of thought, it *is* the life force. A medieval alchemical drawing depicts Adam asleep with the World Tree growing from between his legs. And if the World Tree lies at the center of the Grail Castle, then it grows from the Grail King's loins as well.

Some of our readers may balk at the notion that the healing of the Grail King involves that deeply celebrated and much maligned portion of the male anatomy. And it has been said, albeit rather crassly, that men think with their…well, *you* know. But if we look more closely at this statement without taking immediate offense, we may discover a truth. A man—any man—requires an arena wherein he may fulfill the *natural* urge to assert his energy, initiative, courage, will, and individuality. Natural urges can *not* be satisfied by sitting, first in a car, then in an office, for forty hours a week or more. Nor are they appeased by spending the weekend sitting on the seat of a power mower or golf cart. There is no real meat, nothing to chew, nothing to reward a man, in the undertaking of most mainstream activities. A man needs to hunt, fish, and get dirty. He needs the wide-open spaces and a campfire in the woods. He needs the quiet pursuits of soul-searching, artistry, evoking his own brand of poetry in the soul or on a piece of paper. He needs the occasional rowdy good time with the guys as well as frequent lusty times in the bedchamber with a consenting adult of his choice.

Remember when the spirit was willing and so was the flesh? Accessing the primal self is tantamount to rediscovering the instinctual promptings of the animal soul. Many of us were free and easy with our bodies in our younger days. In time we sobered up, both literally and figuratively. Changing social mores, and finally the AIDS virus, gave us good reasons to withdraw, to reassess our values. For those who were already concerned with some manner of spiritual path, there were other issues as well, notably the many ascetic disciplines which have become increasingly popular and which teach that the flesh must be renounced because the world is *maya* or illusion. Some of the tenets of these ascetic pathways may have helped many people to find a heightened sense of inner self-awareness. However, our inordinate focus on the splendors of the inner life has also forced us into a collective neurosis/psychosis complete with dysfunctional families, friendships, acquaintances, strangers—you name it! We feel separate and it isn't working. Something is wrong. Those who took the inner journey, whether at mid-life or earlier, may have traveled a long way on the road to self-realization, but the quest is not over. We are still searching for that quintessential something which will soothe our souls.

Rigid disciplines, whether Eastern or Western, which include total spiritual and mental control, emotional repression, vegetarianism, and sexual abstinence, may be right for some, but they are not right for everyone. Try as we might to deny it, our personal desires form our connecting link with the natural world, with the poetry in our souls. Spiritual and mental liberation, emotional freedom, the knowledge that all things are sacred, and the ecstasy of sexual union are all important to awakening the Wild Man and evoking poetry in the soul. When we remove ourselves from all "worldly" things (especially sex, which, in the larger sense, exists on all levels—spiritual, mental, emotional, and physical), we create and perpetuate a trend which may very well lead us to annihilation of the species. To do so is to drive through life with the parking brake on or twist the human spirit into the artificial perfection of a bonsai tree.

The idea that we can remove ourselves from the world is separative and exclusive, not unitive and inclusive. Nature is a oneness, a continuum, a unity of all life. The sexual force is a natural function of the life force itself, which is sacred. It is both natural and sacred to experience beauty in the world of form. Nature, the universe with all its phenomena, is the flowering magnificence of the World Tree.

Thus Finn turned his attention not to his "inner self" or "inner child," but outward, toward the world. It was Nature which inspired him. Nature is, and must be, the teacher of all men. We live in a world without mentors; if we are realists, we know full well that no Merlin will ever come to touch us on the brow and fill us with wisdom. We have to catch our own salmon.

We must accomplish this through a continued awareness of Nature. If Cernunnos, the Wild Man, is in fact the original lord of the Grail Kingdom, then we all must go forth to meet him—not always in meditation or introversion, but as often as possible in the *real* world, the world of streams, forests, deserts, and hills. No man can reclaim the wild magic in his soul—what Finn would call *poetry*—if he lacks this contact with Nature.

And if Nature teaches us to discover poetry in the light of a campfire or the smell of pine needles, it must teach us something greater. It must teach us that Nature itself, the world in all its sacredness, needs our attention, our Warrior spirit, and our concern. In myths everywhere, the Wild Man grows into a King. This is the conclusion of the "Iron John" fairytale, as well as of "Beauty and the Beast." The antlers of Cernunnos are there, still intact, beneath the Grail King's royal crown. And it is the business of Kings to act as keepers of the land, caretakers of the greening world.

If we follow the wildness and poetry in our souls into the heart of Nature, Nature will teach us all things. Like all those who have fished for the salmon of wisdom and journeyed to the Grail Castle, we may cast aside our all-too-limited roles of Warrior, Lover, Magician, or even King, and we may become all things, what the Irish sagas call *samildanach*, the "man of many gifts."

There is a tale concerning the god Lugh, the greatest of all Celtic gods, the one called Samildanach.[9] It is said that the Tuatha de Danaan, the Children of Danu, came to Ireland ages ago, and fought with an older, darker race of gods called the Fomorians. But Nuada, King of the Tuatha de Danaan, was wounded in the battle; in fact, he lost an arm. No man who was crippled could become a king, so the kingship went to a Fomorian named Bres.

Bres was a sick king. He gave no gifts, no wine nor even ale, to those who visited his hall. He cared little for the land or those who lived upon it. Ireland became a wasteland. In time, the Tuatha de Danaan won their sacred land back again. They even set Nuada on the throne once again, equipped with a silver hand made by the smith of the gods. But they only won that fight for the land because they acquired the services of a *samildanach*, a man complete and whole.

With his coming, we may conclude our own stories. It is said that Nuada was holding a feast at Tara when the doorkeeper saw a band of warriors coming through the night. Leading them was Lugh, a young warrior of handsome mien, dressed like a king. Lugh approached the doorkeeper and asked for admittance.

"No one enters Tara unless he has an art or skill," said the doorkeeper.

"Question me," said Lugh. "I am a smith."

"We need thee not. We have a smith."

"Question me. I am a harper."

"We need thee not. We have a harper."

"Question me. I am a hero."

"We need thee not. We have a hero."

"Question me. I am a bard."

"We need thee not. We have a bard."

"Question me. I am a Druid."

"We need thee not. We have a Druid."

"Question me. I am a healer."

"We need thee not. We have a healer."

"Ask the king if he has any man with all these skills. If so, I will depart. But if not, then *open the door and let me in!*"

Notes

1. *Rig Veda* 10.97, quoted in Jessie L. Weston, *From Ritual to Romance* (Garden City, NY: Doubleday Anchor Books, 1957), 102–3.

2. Ibid., 106

3. Ibid., 106–9.

4. Ibid., 109.

5. Cross and Slover, *Ancient Irish Tales*, 505.

6. W. B. Yeats, "The Wanderings of Oisin," from *The Collected Poems of W. B. Yeats*, 381.

7. Cross and Slover, op. cit., 355–6.

8. Adapted by Kenneth Johnson from a Gaelic original.

9. Cross and Slover, op. cit., 35–6.

Write Your Own Personal Myth

We have experienced, through our perusal of male myths in the Celtic Tradition, men who have realized their own empowerment. This is why we call them heroes; some of them, even, wear the lineaments of the gods. They have seen their life's purpose, realized their destiny, and fulfilled their heart's desire. Individuality and creative self-expression run strong in their veins. Pwyll, Perceval, Gwydion, Gawain, Manawyddan, Bran, Cuchulain: these archetypal characters teach us to recognize the personal myths and dramas at work in our own daily lives. Are they different from us? Older, perhaps, but not always that much wiser. Each has undergone a process that commingled great pain and exquisite joy. The rewards they received came after much hard work and soul-searching, questing for the meaning of life. The gods and heroes are not different from us in character; they differ only in their determination, persistence, tenacity, and fearless action.

We are part of, not separate from, the great archetypal web that holds the world together. It is therefore important to discover which archetypal patterns and dramas form the unconscious script for our lives. Below, you will find a series of pages that will help you to determine your personal myth. First, begin by mentally reconstructing your life's journey. When you endeavor to do so, you may find that you respond to one of several archetypal patterns. These may be the same ones which emerged from our earlier survey, at the end of Part I. However, it is also true that different archetypes emerge within us from time to time, at different stages of our lives, and this exercise is designed to help you perceive the ebb and flow of the great archetypal tides within you.

When you are ready, write your story down according to your own perception of what occurred. This is very important: you must work from your own perceptions in order to validate your own myth.

The exercise is divided into a group of seven-year cycles, beginning with birth and ending with death—or, more precisely, your own vision of that transition. Cycles of seven years have a traditional resonance in myth, as well as in ancient or "mythic" disciplines such as astrology. During each cycle of seven years we seek, consciously or unconsciously, solutions for the basic issues of our lives. Hence we may find that fundamental patterns and legends in the course of our lives emerge more easily when considered within the context of these seven-year periods.

It may be helpful to divide each seven-year cycle into four aspects of growth and development. These may be labeled as follows: Preparation, Emergence, Ascension, and Climax.

The **Preparation** for any given seven-year period is formed of the events which lead up to it: omens, visions, and events which made us aware that a new era, a new cycle was about to begin.

The **Emergence** may be one event, or many: it indicates the way in which the pattern or characteristic quest motif of that particular cycle came into our consciousness or emerged.

The **Ascension** chronicles the path itself; the triumphs, tragedies and other incidents which form the actual story about our time upon that particular seven-year road. The period of Ascension leads ultimately to…

The **Climax,** which may be either happy or tragic, successful or otherwise, but, in any event, indicates the event (whether or inner or outer) which brought that cycle to a conclusion.

Work with as many seven-year cycles as you have experienced thus far in your life. Though we have not yet experienced death, we may try to imagine how, when, where, and why this natural aspect of life will occur. And for those with a spirit of adventure, a section entitled "Rebirth" has been added following "Death." Use your imagination with this one. If you require more space, begin your own journal.

My Personal Myth

0–7 years

Preparation:

Emergence:

Ascension:

Climax:

7–14 years

Preparation:

Emergence:

Ascension:

Climax:

14–21 years

Preparation:

Emergence:

Ascension:

Climax:

21–28 years

Preparation:

Emergence:

Ascension:

Climax:

28–35 years

Preparation:

Emergence:

Ascension:

Climax:

35–42 years

Preparation:

Emergence:

Ascension:

Climax:

42–49 years

Preparation:

Emergence:

Ascension:

Climax:

49–56 years

Preparation:

Emergence:

Ascension:

Climax:

56–63 years

Preparation:

Emergence:

Ascension:

Climax:

63–70 years

Preparation:

Emergence:

Ascension:

Climax:

70–77 years

Preparation:

Emergence:

Ascension:

Climax:

77–84 years

Preparation:

Emergence:

Ascension:

Climax:

Death (describe how you envision your own death)

Rebirth (who you will become)

Index

STAY IN TOUCH

On the following pages you will find listed, with their current prices, some of the books now available on related subjects. Your book dealer stocks most of these and will stock new titles in the Llewellyn series as they become available. We urge your patronage.

To obtain our full catalog, to keep informed about new titles as they are released and to benefit from informative articles and helpful news, you are invited to write for our bimonthly news magazine/catalog, *Llewellyn's New Worlds of Mind and Spirit*. A sample copy is free, and it will continue coming to you at no cost as long as you are an active mail customer. Or you may subscribe for just $10.00 in U.S.A. and Canada ($20.00 overseas, first class mail). Many bookstores also have *New Worlds* available to their customers. Ask for it.

Stay in touch! In *New Worlds'* pages you will find news and features about new books, tapes and services, announcements of meetings and seminars, articles helpful to our readers, news of authors, products and services, special money-making opportunities, and much more.

Llewellyn's New Worlds of Mind and Spirit
P.O. Box 64383-K369, St. Paul, MN 55164-0383, U.S.A.

* * *

TO ORDER BOOKS AND TAPES

If your book dealer does not have the books described on the following pages readily available, you may order them direct from the publisher by sending full price in U.S. funds, plus $3.00 for postage and handling for orders *under* $10.00; $4.00 for orders *over* $10.00. There are no postage and handling charges for orders over $50.00. Postage and handling rates are subject to change. UPS Delivery: We ship UPS whenever possible. Delivery guaranteed. Provide your street address as UPS does not deliver to P.O. Boxes. UPS to Canada requires a $50.00 minimum order. Allow 4-6 weeks for delivery. Orders outside the U.S.A. and Canada: Airmail—add retail price of book; add $5.00 for each non-book item (tapes, etc.); add $1.00 per item for surface mail.

FOR GROUP STUDY AND PURCHASE

Because there is a great deal of interest in group discussion and study of the subject matter of this book, we feel that we should encourage the adoption and use of this particular book by such groups by offering a special quantity price to group leaders or agents.

Our Special Quantity Price for a minimum order of five copies of *The Grail Castle* is $36.00 cash-with-order. This price includes postage and handling within the United States. Minnesota residents must add 6.5% sales tax. For additional quantities, please order in multiples of five. For Canadian and foreign orders, add postage and handling charges as above. Credit card (VISA, MasterCard, American Express) orders are accepted. Charge card orders only may be phoned in free within the U.S.A. or Canada by dialing 1-800-THE-MOON. For customer service, call 1-612-291-1970. Mail orders to:

LLEWELLYN PUBLICATIONS
P.O. Box 64383-K369, St. Paul, MN 55164-0383, U.S.A.

Prices subject to change without notice.

MYTHIC ASTROLOGY
Archetypal Powers in the Horoscope
Ariel Guttman & Kenneth Johnson

Here is an entirely new dimension of self-discovery based on understanding the mythic archetypes represented in the astrological birth chart. Myth has always been closely linked with astrology; all our planets are named for the Graeco-Roman deities and derive their interpretative meanings from them. To richly experience the myths which lie at the heart of astrology is to gain a deeper and more spiritual perspective on the art of astrology and on life itself.

Mythic Astrology is unique because it allows the reader to explore the connection between astrology and the spirituality of myth in depth, without the necessity of a background in astrology, anthropology or the classics. This book is an important contribution to the continuing study of mythology as a form of New Age spirituality and is also a reference work of enduring value. Students of mythology, the Goddess, art, history, Jungian psychological symbolism and literature—as well as lovers of astrology—will all enjoy the text and numerous illustrations.

0-87542-248-9, 382 pgs., 7 x 10, 100 illus., softcover **$17.95**

Prices subject to change without notice.